D0586000

THE OMBUDSMAN PLAN

The Worldwide
Spread of an Idea
Revised Second Edition

Donald C. Rowat

Professor of Political Science
Carleton University
Ottawa, Canada

UNIVERSITY
PRESS OF
AMERICA

LANHAM • NEW YORK • LONDON

First edition published by McClelland and Stewart Limited, Toronto,
1973. Revised edition in Japanese to be published by Waseda
University Press, Tokyo (copyright held by Carleton University
Press, Ottawa).

Library of Congress Cataloging in Publication Data

Rowat, Donald Cameron.
  The ombudsman plan.

  Bibliography: p.
  Includes index.
  1. Ombudsman.   I. Title.
JF1525.045R68   1985   350'.91   85-22772
ISBN 0-8191-5039-8 (alk. paper)
ISBN 0-8191-5040-1 (pbk. : alk. paper)

CONTENTS

The Scandinavian countries, long regarded as models of democratic government, have originated a unique agency of government: a special parliamentary officer known as the ombudsman, which might be translated loosely as citizens'
defender, grievance man or public watchdog. His job is to
receive complaints from citizens about the way in which they
have been treated by government officials, to investigate
these complaints and, where he finds them justified, to
propose a remedy. When remedial action is not taken, he can
publicize the case and report on it to parliament.

The office of ombudsman has enjoyed a remarkable spread
throughout the world in recent years. In 1955 only three
Scandinavian countries--Sweden, Finland and Denmark--had an
ombudsman. In 1962 two more countries--Norway and New Zeal-
and--adopted the plan. New Zealand's adoption paved the way
for its early spread to other Commonwealth countries and the
United States. It was adopted by Guyana in 1966, and by the
United Kingdom, two Canadian provinces and the American
state of Hawaii in 1967. After that, the plan spread more
rapidly, to both developed and developing countries.

By mid-1983 there were 21 national plans in operation
that had been classified by the International Ombudsman
Institute as general legislative ombudsman offices.[1] In
addition, national plans had been recently adopted but not
yet implemented in three other countries, for a total of 24
national adoptions. Also, one or more general offices had
been adopted at the state or regional level in six additional countries. In all, 89 general plans had been adopted
at the national, state or local level in 31 countries around
the world. Of these, 24 were national, 44 were state or
regional, and 21 were local. In addition, general plans had
been officially proposed but not yet adopted in several
other countries. There were also many specialized ombudsman
offices at the national, state or local level in several
countries, and the idea had spread to school systems, universities, hospitals, welfare homes and non-governmental
organizations.

The reason is that the rise of the welfare state in the modern world has resulted in a rapid and bewildering growth of bureaucracies. This has made necessary new protections against bureaucratic bungling and abuses of power. The ombudsman is a novel and uniquely appropriate institution for dealing with the average citizen's complaints about unfair administrative action. It differs from the traditional methods of handling individual grievances and has important advantages over these methods.

What is the nature of the original ombudsman system? Why is it needed elsewhere? Can it be easily transferred? What conclusions may be drawn regarding the adoption of the ombudsman plan elsewhere? Finally, why and how has the idea spread so rapidly throughout the world? What advantages does the office have over similar complaint-handling agencies? These are some of the questions to be explored in this book.

I could see the importance of the ombudsman as a unique mechanism of democratic control over bureaucracy when I made my first study of the office in 1960. I immediately began writing about it and advocating its adoption in Canada and other democratic countries. Besides editing a comprehensive book on the subject, The Ombudsman: Citizen's Defender (1965), with essays written by many experts, including several ombudsmen, I have over the years written a number of pieces of my own. In 1968 a second edition of The Ombudsman was published, for which I wrote a preface on new developments and added new ombudsman acts and bills to the appendix, but the body of the book could not be updated because of its multiple authorship. Yet the idea has continued to spread rapidly, and many new developments have taken place about which those interested in the ombudsman idea should know.

It therefore occurred to me that my own writings could be put together, updated and revised as a short book on the subject. Allen and Unwin, and the University of Toronto Press, kindly gave me permission to reproduce portions from my own contributions to the earlier book. The present book is thus a collection of my previous writings but revised so that they fit together into a logical whole and so as to stress the most recent developments in the rapid spread of the ombudsman idea. It is intended as a short, up-to-date review of the subject for both laymen and scholars. Serious scholars of the subject may also wish to consult the earlier book.

The first edition of the present book was published in 1973, and was well enough received to encourage me to prepare a revised edition. This second edition, which is also being published in Japanese by Waseda University Press, Tokyo, is basically the same as the first edition, except that it has been extended and updated to take account of the many developments around the world since 1973. Also, I have added to the Conclusion a discussion of the five basic requirements for a successful plan.

The first edition had a very long Appendix, which contained my reviews of books on the ombudsman, an extensive bibliography, examples of provisions for local and university ombudsmen, and ombudsman laws, constitutional provisions and proposals that had appeared since 1968. Since this material is now dated and may be too specialized for the average reader, it was omitted from the present edition. Serious scholars interested in this material may consult the first edition, which can still be ordered from Carleton University Press, Ottawa.

I should like to acknowledge my debt to the Canada Council and its successor, the Social Sciences and Humanities Research Council of Canada, for several senior fellowships and research grants, without which I would never have been able to do my research and writing on the subject, and to thank the publishers of my earlier works on the ombudsman for permission to reprint portions from these works. Nor should I forget the scholars and ombudsmen around the world who took time from their busy schedules to send me information.

vi

In the preparation of this edition, I should like to thank Bernard Frank and Randall Ivany, of the International Ombudsman Institute, for providing information on new developments. In updating the book, I have relied heavily on the IOI's invaluable annual survey of developments around the world (see Bibliography).

In recent years there have been few innovations in the machinery of democratic government comparable to the earlier invention of the secret ballot and the public corporation. The rapid spread of the ombudsman plan around the world indicates that it is an important new addition to the devices for democratic control of a bureaucracy. It can be adapted easily to either parliamentary or congressional government, and is already operating successfully in many democratic countries. I hope that the readers will give serious consideration to its unique characteristics. The most important of these is its independence from the executive, mainly achieved by providing for it by law and making it an arm of the legislature.

Donald C. Rowat
January 1985

Footnote - Preface

1. See <u>Ombudsman and other Complaint-Handling Systems Survey</u>, Vol. XI, July 1, 1982 - June 30, 1983 (Edmonton, International Ombudsman Institute, 1983), Chs. V,X. The other figures in this paragraph were compiled from the same source.

PART ONE:
THE FIRST
OMBUDSMAN SYSTEMS

1.

THE OMBUDSMEN IN SWEDEN

Ombudsman was originally a Swedish word meaning a representative or agent of the people or a group of people. Since the word is still used in this general sense in Sweden, there are several kinds of ombudsmen in that country, but as used in other countries the word refers specifically to the Swedish Justitieombudsman, the officer appointed by the legislature to handle complaints against administrative and judicial action. In the English-speaking world this term was at first translated, usually as "parliamentary commissioner for the administration," and this is the formal title used in the legislation creating the office in New Zealand and Britain. But as the idea came to be more widely discussed in other countries, the single word ombudsman has now been adopted in most languages to describe the office. In English the word is coming more and more to be pronounced in its Anglicized version, with the accent on the middle syllable (to rhyme with "woodsman").

Though the ombudsman plan is new in the sense that it helps to meet the problem of an expanded bureaucracy in the modern welfare state, it is actually an old institution in Sweden. The Justitieombudsman was first appointed as an officer of the legislature under the constitution of 1809. His functions of receiving complaints from the people and protecting them against injustice were performed even before that date by an officer appointed by the king - the chancellor of justice. When the legislature reasserted its independence from the executive in 1809, it decided to appoint an ombudsman as its own "defender of the law." While the chancellor still exists and continues to receive complaints directly from the public, he has other important administrative duties, and the ombudsman became by far the most important officer for receiving, investigating and remedying complaints.

In the 19th century, the ombudsman's activities were mainly concerned with supervising the courts and the police, but the growth of administration in the 20th century shifted his emphasis to the bureaucracy. In 1915 his docket became so heavy that a separate ombudsman, the Militieombudsman, was appointed for the armed services. Further growth in the work load has resulted in an important change in the Swedish system.   In 1965 a governmental committee had recommended that, in order to reduce the load on the ombudsman for civil affairs, the supervision of judges, prison officials and police should be transferred to the ombudsman for military affairs.   As an alternative solution, Mr. Bexelius, the renowned ombudsman for civil affairs, proposed a system of three ombudsmen to divide among themselves the tasks of the two existing ombudsmen. Early in 1967 the government introduced a bill in which these proposals were set forth.   Since it is up to parliament alone to decide about its own ombudsmen, the government did not make any recommendation on which solution should be preferred.   Parliament decided in favour of the Bexelius proposal, and in 1968 created a system of three ombudsmen.

In 1976 this system was again reorganized to provide for four ombudsmen, and for one of them to be named the administrative head who decides the main orientation of activities. They have a common office and staff of assistants, but each specializes in a different field and decides his own cases independently.   The administrative head is in charge of taxation and the execution of judgments.   A second ombudsman supervises the courts, public prosecutors, police and prisons.   A third handles social welfare and education, while the fourth supervises the armed forces and all other matters.

Nature of Ombudsman Institution

The ombudsman institution as developed in Sweden has a number of unusual features which, in combination, makes it unique among grievance-handling, appeal and investigating bodies.   First, an ombudsman is an officer of the legislature and not of the exective.   He (or she)[1] is appointed by the legislature and is free to report back to it at any time. The four ombudsmen jointly place before it a published annual report which describes and comments on important cases. This report is considered and acted upon by a standing committee of the legislature.

Second, an ombudsman is an impartial investigator and is politically independent, even of the legislature. His office is provided for in the constitution, and once he has begun the investigation of a case the legislators do not intervene. By tradition, all important political parties agree on his appointment.   Although he is appointed for a four-year term, he is frequently reappointed for a second or third term.

4

Third, a significant limitation upon an ombudsman's power is that, unlike the courts, he has no right to quash or reverse a decision and has no direct control over the courts or administration. He has only the power to investigate and, where an injustice is found, to propose a remedy. His influence is based upon his objectivity, competence, superior knowledge and prestige. When his proposed remedy is not accepted by the authorities, his main weapon to secure remedial action is publicicity--through his reports to the legislature and through the press. He does, however, have the power to prosecute officials for illegal acts. Although this power is seldom used nowadays, the fact of its existence has no doubt increased the ombudsman's influence.

Fourth, he has power to investigate on his own initiative. He can inspect courts and administrative agencies and can take up cases based on reports in the press. Evidence of the importance of these powers is that many of the ombudsmen's most important cases, requiring a prosecution or change in administrative practice or law, arise in this way.

Fifth, his method of handling appeals against administrative decisions is--unlike that of the courts--direct, informal, speedy and cheap. All that is required to initiate an appeal is for the complainant to write a letter. As an added protection for the large number of inmates of state institutions now found in the modern welfare state, letters from inmates of prisons, welfare homes and mental hospitals must be sent to him unopened by the supervisory staff. No formal court-like hearings are held, and an ombudsman's work is done almost entirely by mail. He requests and studies departmental documents and, if not satisfied that a complaint is unwarranted, requests a departmental explanation. If the explanation is unsatisfactory, he will reprimand the official and try to secure remedial action. Where necessary, he will also recommend changes in laws and regulations designed to remove injustices and anomalies. Because their method of handling grievances is so informal and simple, the four ombudsmen have a surprisingly small budget and staff.

An important feature of the ombudsman system is that, because of the simple and cheap way in which complaints are handled, many minor complaints can be satisfied. Though important to the claimant, they would not be worth the cost of an elaborate court procedure. Many cases involve no more than explaining to the bewildered citizen the reasons for the decision of which he has complained, and warning the government office in question that in future it should give adequate reasons for its decisions. Other examples of minor grievances are complaints about getting no answer to an

5

application, leisureliness in replying to mail, giving insufficient information on a right of appeal, and delay in
making decisions. Nevertheless, some of the ombudsmen's
most valuable work has been done on serious cases of illegality involving the liberty of the subject, such as the un-
justifiable use of handcuffs, or the recording of telephone
conversations by the police, or an assault by a nurse on a
mental patient. As a result of an ombudsman's investigations, he may direct a department to discipline one or more
of its officers, or in more serious cases, he may prosecute
in the courts an officer who has taken unlawful action.

Another unusual feature is the ombudsmen's power to
oversee the courts. A few years ago, for instance, as a
result of investigating a complaint, the civilian ombudsman
prosecuted a judge for insulting a witness and calling him a
liar. The judge was fined $300.

Proof that even in well-administered countries like
Sweden supposedly responsible officials do indeed abuse
their power is that over the years some very senior officials, including heads of royal boards, have had to be
prosecuted by the Swedish ombudsmen. A recent example was
the prosecution of a police chief and the public prosecutor
of a county for illegally confiscating a fisherman's boat.
There were even three occasions in the 19th century when
parliament directed the Justitieombudsman to prosecute cabinet ministers, though otherwise ministers are excluded from
the ombudsmen's supervision.

The ombudsmen feel that they have a special responsibility for questions concerning the liberty of the citizen--in
particular arrest and detention. The detention of citizens
in the impressive variety of modern state institutions, such
as jails, prisons, correction and welfare homes and mental
hospitals, may easily involve the wrongful deprivation of
liberty. For instance, in 1955, the civilian ombudsman had
to prosecute a county governor for wrongfully detaining a
chronic alcoholic.

Since the Swedish ombudsmen's power to initiate investigations on their own is used so frequently and is so important, let me give an example of this in some detail. It is a
case that occurred just before I visited Mr. Bexelius, then
the civilian ombudsman, in 1960. Mr. Bexelius told me that
one day, while scanning newspaper reports of court cases, he
came across a story in which a reporter was discussing the
case of a young ruffian who had been put in jail for some
minor offence. The reporter casually mentioned that this
young fellow must have been well educated, because he had

written his girl friend a very literate love letter, which the reporter had read in the police files. Mr. Bexelius told me that when he read this story, his eyes popped. "What was this poor fellow's love letter doing in the police files, available to be read, and perhaps even published, by an inquisitive reporter?" According to Swedish law, though officials have the right to censor any inmate's mail, they must not intercept it and place it on file, except for special reasons. So Mr. Bexelius wrote to the official in question and asked for an explanation. The official replied that the letter had been in the files because the police suspected the inmate of forgery and needed a copy of his handwriting. The ombudsman felt that this explanation was acceptable and took no further action. But he told me that if the letter had got into the files by mistake, he would certainly have reprimanded the official in question.

Some idea of the nature and extent of an ombudsman's work may be obtained by considering the number and disposition of the cases dealt with. Before the change to three ombudsmen in 1968, the military ombudsman handled about 650 cases a year. Most of these arose from his own investigations and fewer than 100 were based on individual complaints. The civilian ombudsman, on the other hand, received about 1200 complaints a year, and in addition initiated about 200 inquiries of his own. By 1980-81, the total number of cases handled by the four ombudsmen had risen to 3456, of which 501, or nearly 15 per cent, required remedial action. Only 91 were initiated by the ombudsmen themselves, but 65 of these, or more than two-thirds, resulted in criticisms of official action.

Sample Cases From Sweden

A better understanding of the nature of the cases with which an ombudsman deals, and of the way in which he handles them, may be gained by reviewing in some detail a number of specific investigations, and noting the action taken. Here are some important cases chosen and presented in person by Mr. Bexelius to a subcommittee of the American Senate in 1966:

Supervision of police - (i) A man who was a habitual drunkard had, when drunk, maltreated his wife, who had been unfaithful to him. The wife went to the police, and the police--since the police doctor had examined him--sent the man to a mental hospital where he was detained for eight months. Then he complained to me. When I examined the hopital records, I couldn't find reason to believe that the man was mentally ill. Therefore, I wrote to the Central Board of Health--the highest medical society in Sweden--and asked for their opinion. They answered that there had not been sufficient reasons to detain the man in a mental hospital against his will. Of course, the man could and ought to have been taken to a home for habitual drunkards but there he would not have been detained for more than three or four months. I didn't find reasons for prosecuting the doctor, but I wrote to the Government and asked them to give the man compensation.

(ii) In the summer of 1963, two young girls were killed in Stockholm within a few weeks of each other by a sexual murderer. During the investigation carried out after the first crime, but before the second one, several tips were received from the public charging a certain man who was also interrogated by the police without, however, being found out until after the second murder. Critical viewpoints on the investigation were brought out in the press. I therefore found it necessary to make an investigation, and two members of my staff heard all the policemen who had worked on this case. On the basis of the findings of this investigation, I found cause for criticism of the work of the police. In particular, the number of persons taking part in the investigation had been too limited, and the system adopted for filing of the many items of information received from the public had not worked.

In this serious case, the Chief of Police should have more actively supervised the organization of the operation. It seemed all but incredible that the criminal had not been exposed earlier to prevent the second murder. The defects found in the work of the police in the course of this investigation led to the preparation of efficient plans for how the police were to operate in similar cases. This action proved to be of positive value for future work of the police in their duties to protect the general public.

Official Conflict of Interest - In December 1961 the president of a private charter airline arranged a goodwill trip by air from Sweden to Paris called "The Christmas Shopping trip." Through reports in the press I was informed about the fact that government officials had taken part in the trip. On my request, the matter was investigated. Participants in the trip were inter alia, the Director of the Civil Aviation Inspectorate and his wife. Before the trip, the Director had submitted the question of his participation to his superior, the Director-General of the National Swedish Board of

8

Civil Aviation, who gave him permission to take part in the trip. I found that the Director of the Civil Aviation Inspectorate had obviously been invited because of his official position. There was, though, no evidence of the assumption that he had allowed the exercise of his official duties to be influenced by the favor received. In view of the fact that his official duties covered inspecting and controlling functions against the company, he should not have accepted the invitation. By taking part in the trip with his wife, he had acted in a way which was likely to impair public confidence in the exercise of his official duties. By giving the other official permission to participate in the trip, the Director-General of the National Board of Civil Aviation has been neglectful of what, in the nature of his position, had been his duty in his capacity as head of the agency. The two officials were prosecuted and fines imposed. The decision was upheld by the Supreme Court of Sweden.

Judges and Courts - (i) A court had unjustly ordered an arrested person to pay the costs of his own return from the United States to Sweden for trial. The party complained to the Ombudsman on another aspect of the case. But, in his review, the Ombudsman discovered that the complainant had been wrongly made to pay his own transportation costs. Since the law was not clear in regard to the obligation to repay transportation costs, the judge could not be held responsible for the error. But the Ombudsman wrote to the Government and requested that the man be reimbursed. This request was granted.

(ii) The biggest enquiry which I have undertaken concerned the application by the courts of the laws on drunken driving. In Sweden it is an offence to drive a car if the alcohol content of the driver's blood is higher than 0.5 per mille at the time he is driving. In most cases, however, the blood test is taken some hours after the driving. This means that the courts have to estimate on the basis of the blood test how high the alcohol content was when the person was driving. In the courts this is called "calculating backwards." In the course of inspections, I noticed that when making these calculations the courts quite often started out from fallacious assumptions. In the scrutiny, the services of two prominent experts were used and with their aid it was shown how these "back calculations" ought to be made on a proper scientific basis. This enquiry, which was published in the annual report, has undoubtedly been useful in the courts.

9

<u>The Case of the Misplaced Grave</u> - It happened a few
years ago that a farmer was buried in a churchyard in
the country. It was during the winter when the ground
was covered with snow and it was difficult for the digger to find the family grave. A few weeks after the
burial, the daughter of the farmer came to the rector of
the parish and said that she was afraid that her father's coffin had been placed outside the family grave;
and the rector went to the digger, but the digger said
that he had not committed any fault; and then the daughter, who was a waitress, asked the municipal parish
council for permission to investigate through digging,
but the municipal council said "No."
    Then she appealed in the ordinary way to the county
board and there the governor of the county said "No."
And so, she appealed to the Royal Cabinet. And the minister concerned asked the Bishop and the Bishop said
"No." And then the Cabinet said "No." Then she quar-
relled with all the authorities concerned for many
years, but they always said "No."

    Then she complained to the Ombudsman. I sent that
complaint to the municipal parish council and asked for
information, but they didn't have much to say. Then I
ordered the police to ask all persons who could give
information. When I had got this information, I couldn't
say with security if the coffin has been placed outside
the family grave or not. But the circumstances were such
that the parish council ought to have ordered an investigation through digging. The Ombudsman has no power to
order digging in a churchyard. So, I couldn't do any-
thing else than criticize the parish council because
they had not made a real investigation in this case.
But, the waitress took my decision and she went straight
to the Cabinet Minister and said, "Look here, Mr. Minister, here you see the Ombudsman says that there are
reasons for investigation through digging," and so the
Cabinet Council had nothing else to do than order an
investigation through digging. When they dug, they found
that the coffin had been placed outside the family grave.
You can say that this case is a very small one, and it
doesn't matter where that coffin was placed. But for
the daughter, the case was of great importance, and even
for all Swedes it is important to feel that they can get
justice, even if the prestige of a Governor and a Bishop
and a Cabinet Minister is involved.

This last case is more typical of the great bulk of cases
with which an ombudsman deals, and of the way in which he
can secure remedial action on individual grievances. Many

of them seem to be of little significance, yet are of great importance for the peace of mind of the complainant.

The following case, taken from the annual report of the ombudsmen for 1980-81, is an interesting illustration of the many important cases in which the ombudsmen find that a complaint is not justified and thus exonerate the accused officials:

The Case of the Fallen Bridge - On January 18, 1980, at 1:30 a.m., a vessel sailed in thick fog into the 500 m long, 40 m high Almö bridge between the mainland and the island of Tjörn off the Swedish west coast. Before the approach roads had been blocked, six passenger cars and a lorry plunged into the water. Eight people were killed. In the complaint to the Ombudsman it was questioned whether, owing to incompetence and lack of imagination on the part of the police, they had not been too slow in setting up barriers. From the investigation that was made, it appeared that the first reports of the accident received by the police did not state that the bridge had collapsed. Only 20 minutes after the accident did it become clear what had happened. The approach road from the mainland side was blocked off at about the same time by a police patrol. That from the Tjörn side was closed at about 2:20 a.m. by a customs officer who had been put ashore from a coast-guard boat. Part of the criticism directed against the police related to the delay in setting up this road-block. Ombudsman Wigelius' finding, however, was that no policeman involved on the occasion could be blamed for the catastrophic consequences of the collapse of the bridge, but that the police had done a good job under the stressful conditions that prevailed. He also stated that in the prevailing situation there did not appear to have been any real possibility for the police to arrange a road-block in time to limit the extent of the accident.

In summing up the nature of the ombudsman system, Ombudsman Bexelius stressed the following points:

One important aspect of the Ombudsman's activity which is often overlooked is the rejection of unwarranted complaints. Obviously it is of great interest to the official attacked that accusations of abuse are not left open, and that it is made evident by an impartial agency that the complaints were not justified. Also, it is of great importance that accusations made in the press regarding abuse by the authorities are taken up for investigation by an agency free of bureaucratic influence and that these investigations are available and the true facts made known to the general public. By the rejection of unwarranted complaints after proper investigation and on grounds clearly stated, the Ombudsman contributes to strengthening public confidence in the authorities and thus to a feeling of well-being in the society.

It should be emphasized that the office, by its mere existence, counteracts tendencies to transgressions of authority and abuse of powers...The citizens have become increasingly dependent on public agencies. The need for a body independent of the bureaucracy for controlling the growing administration has therefore become more and more evident...

It is...an expression for real democracy that the society keeps an institution with the task to protect the citizens against the society's own organs and that everybody in the society--even if he is poor and without social position--has the right to have his complaint against an authority investigated and tried by an impartial agency. [2]

Footnotes - Chapter One

1. For the sake of brevity, only the masculine form will be used henceforth, but of course should be taken to include the feminine where appropriate.

2. U.S. Congress, Senate, Committee on the Judiciary, Sub-Committee on Administrative Practice and Procedure, Ombudsman (March 7, 1966), 11-12. The cases quoted are found at pp. 7-16 and 33-36.

2.

FINLAND'S DEFENDERS OF THE LAW

Until recently, not much was known in the English-speaking world about the office of the ombudsman in the Nordic countries. Although Sweden had had the office since 1809 and Finland since 1919, it was only after its creation in Denmark in 1955 and adoption in Norway and New Zealand in 1962, that we began to realize its significance as a bulwark of democratic government against the tyranny of officialdom.

In the early 1960s, arising out of Britain's Crichel Down case and the Franks Report, much was written about the need for a similar institution in Britain, and interest in the subject began rising elsewhere in the English-speaking world. Because of language barriers, however, much of what we knew about the office came from the pen of Professor Stephan Hurwitz, the first ombudsman in Denmark, and related only to that country. It is true that the offices in both Denmark and Sweden, and also the closely related office of chancellor of justice in Sweden, had been admirably described in a chapter of Brian Chapman's book on the public services of Europe.[1] But Chapman devoted only a few paragraphs to Finland's ombudsman and chancellor of justice, and very little was known in the English speaking world about these important institutions until after I wrote an article on them in 1961 and Mikael Hiden's book on the Finnish ombudsman had appeared in 1973.[2] Since they differ considerably from the comparable offices in Sweden, and since there is a growing awareness in the common-law countries of the need for more protection against administrative arbitrariness, I believe that some valuable lessons can be learned from a more detailed consideration of their history and present operation.[3]

Finland has had a long history of constitutionalism and tenacious opposition to arbitrary authority, going back more than 700 years. For about 600 years Finland was under Swedish rule and, of course, developed much the same governmental traditions. In 1809 Finland came under Russian rule for more than 100 years, but because it was incorporated as an autonomous state within the Russian Empire, it preserved its judicial and constitutional system virtually intact, until the turn of the century. Then, as Professor Kastari has observed:

When oppressive measures for Russification began, the small Finnish nation had only her own laws and constitution as a means of resistance, and they were desperately upheld, even to the very last. In the course of this unequal battle, a deep respect for the law and the constitution became firmly implanted in the Finnish people, and this respect is even today the most important socio-psychological factor upon which the functioning of the system of fundamental rights is founded.[4]

Because of this bitter experience with Russian attempts at oppression, it is not surprising that the Constitution Act of 1919, creating Finland as a republic, included institutions designed to protect the citizens against the arbitrary rule of officials.

The Chancellor of Justice

It is often assumed that Finland's chancellor of justice is the same as Sweden's. But this is a mistake. He is a much more independent and powerful officer, and is even more important than the Finnish ombudsman as a defender of the law. This has come about because of Finland's unusual history: When the Russian Emperor conquered Finland in 1809, he not only promised to maintain the constitutional laws which had been in force under Swedish rule but also accepted the proposal for an attorney general, similar to the Swedish chancellor of justice, as the highest guardian of the law in the state. He was given power to see that the law was observed by all officials, even the Emperor's own governor general, and to report to the Emperor if they departed from it. Whereas in Sweden the chancellor of justice gradually came under the influence of the cabinet with the development of responsible government, and the parliamentary ombudsman assumed many of his functions, in Finland the attorney general became more and more powerful and independent as a bulwark against Russian domination.

Decisive in this evolution was the appointment as first attorney general of the most famous jurist in Finland at the time, Professor Mathias Colonius, who had been a member of the Swedish supreme court and had published highly esteemed juridical works. During his term the position took on the main characteristics that it still retains, over 160 years later.

When the period of czarist oppression began, at the end of the last century, the position of attorney general became a very difficult one. Since their armed services had been abolished, the Finns had nothing to rely on but their traditional legal barricades, from behind which they fought a gallant but losing battle: Finnish courts refused to apply Russian laws which were not in accordance with Finnish constitutional laws and had not been passed by the Finnish diet. But such stubbornness resulted in reprisals, one of the most severe being the arrest of the whole superior court of Viipuri--about twenty persons--who were taken before a Russian court of law in St. Petersburg, removed from office, and sentenced to prison. A focal point of the battle, of course, was the office of attorney general. Finnish attorneys general who refused to obey the Russians were dismissed by the Emperor. On the other hand, those considered too submissive were hated and opposed by the Finns. By 1905 the situation had become so serious that the attorney general was assassinated by a Finn, and later another met the same fate.

The actions of P.S. Svinhufvud, who later became the first prime minister and then president of the new republic, neatly demonstrate the importance that Finns attached to constitutional precedent and to the office of attorney general as defender of the law. In 1905 Svinhufvud acted as attorney for the defence at the trial of the attorney general's assassin, and in 1914, as a judge, he refused to send the attorney general, who was by then a Russian, a copy of certain minutes of a court of law on the ground that the attorney general, since he was not a Finnish jurist, had been illegally appointed. Because of this refusal Svinhufvud was arrested by the Russians and imprisoned in Siberia until the revolution occurred three years later. Immediately after the revolution he was released from prison and was himself appointed as attorney general.

When the Constitution of 1919 was adopted the office of attorney general was continued. The name was changed to chancellor of justice, but the powers and duties of the office remained much the same. Although the Finns no longer had to oppose a foreign czar, and had created their own executive institutions--the president and the council of ministers - they were by now profoundly suspicious of executive and official powers of all kinds, and did not hesitate to create ample checks upon its exercise. This, then, explains the preservation of the powerful office of chancellor of justice, as part of the executive, and the creation of the overlapping and almost duplicate office of ombudsman under the legislature.

It is true that the chancellor of justice may be considered part of the executive, in the sense that he is appointed by the president of the republic. But with the strong support of tradition and in accordance with the careful distribution of powers written into the 1919 constitution, he is genuinely independent, even to the point of having power to take proceedings against the president himself. The most remarkable power of the chancellor is that of actually supervising the president and the cabinet to ensure that they take no unconstitutional or illegal action. To this end he attends all meetings of the cabinet and of the president's council (separate meetings of the council of ministers, chaired by the president). It is sometimes assumed that because he attends their meetings, the chancellor acts simply as another member of the council. But this is not so. His role is that of a watchdog - well symbolized, for those who have seen the Finnish council chambers, by the fact that during meetings of the cabinet or of the president's council he does not sit with the ministers but instead back from the council table, in a kind of lonely eminence. If they refuse to take his advice on a question of legality, he may divulge the matter publicly in his published annual reports to the president and to the diet. The chancellor has seldom had to take this action, however, simply because the president, the prime minister and the other ministers know that it can be taken, and usually accept his advice. It is no part of the chancellor's duty, of course, to advise on a matter of policy. His job is purely and simply to ensure that proposed laws and official actions are constitutional, legal, and in accordance with natural justice.

To fortify his position as defender of the law, Finland's chancellor of justice, unlike Sweden's, has been made supreme prosecutor of the country. His orders have to be obeyed by all other prosecutors, and he even has the right to prosecute, before a special high court of impeachment, not only members of the supreme court and the supreme administrative court but also members of the cabinet. He may even, in case of treason, prosecute the president of the republic before the supreme court. But to prevent him from becoming too powerful, the president may, in accordance with the subtle system of checks and balances created by the 1919 Constitution, dismiss the chancellor if he feels this to be justified, and the chancellor himself may be indicted before the high court. If either the diet or the president believes that he has been acting against the law, he may be prosecuted before it by the ombudsman or by someone designated by the president. So far, however, this has never happened.

Proof that the chancellor's extensive powers are desirable and indeed may have to be used, is that in 1960, on the basis of a complaint by two members of the diet and a full investigation, he found it necessary to prosecute several of the directors and officials of a government insurance company that had, among other things, granted loans too freely to government officials. As a result, the court of appeals handed out stiff fines for most of the officials, including the president of the supreme administrative court and the prime minister. Although the case was appealed to the supreme court, this forced the resignation of the prime minister and required the formation of a new Agrarian cabinet. Results such as these indicate the importance of the chancellor's office.

The chancellor also has the right to demand cancellation of a court judgment which had already acquired legal force if in his opinion an obvious error has been made or new evidence has turned up. An interesting example involved the supreme court in cancelling a divorce, after it had been ascertained that the husband and wife had submitted false information. To satisfy the legal requirement for a divorce, they had claimed that they had lived apart for two years. The actual reason for the divorce was that the wife was guilty of embezzlement and the husband, being a military officer of high social standing, wanted to divorce his wife before her crime was revealed. After the chancellor's revelation of the new evidence, both husband and wife were prosecuted.

The Chancellor and the Ombudsman

Except that the ombudsman is an officer of the legislature, is appointed by it for a four-year term, and reports only to it, his office and powers are much the same as those of the chancellor. Like the chancellor, his job is to see that all official and judicial actions are within the law, and to receive complaints from any aggrieved citizens who believe otherwise. He has the same power to supervise and be informed about acts and decisions of the council of ministers, and to prosecute high officials, including judges and ministers, and indeed has prosecuted several ministers in recent years. Like the chancellor, he may initiate investigations on his own, make inspections, demand information, papers or documents, report to the diet, and propose changes in the law and regulations designed to make them more equitable. Moreover, the regulations for his office state that his salary shall be determined on the same basis as that of the chancellor.

Because of its history, however, and the fact that the chancellor is also chief prosecutor, the chancellor's office tends to overshadow that of the ombudsman. For example, though the ombudsman has the right to attend meetings of the council of ministers, he does not do so, and his power to prosecute does not extend to the president of the republic. Added to the strength of tradition is the fact that the chancellor, in his capacity as chief prosecutor, also receives the complaints of one citizen against another. Often citizens do not make the distinction between an injury by another citizen and one by a government official. In their minds the office of chancellor has become the place to lodge any complaint. Hence, many complaints about official action are still received by the chancellor.

In 1933, however, as a result of the growing load upon the chancellor, and to provide some kind of division of labour, it was provided that he should hand over to the ombudsman complaints from prisoners and soldiers. Since many complaints are in this category, much of the load of investigating complaints was thus removed from the chancellor's shoulders. Also, the main burden of inspections has been taken over by the ombudsman, who every year inspects a selection of prisons, other state institutions, government offices, administrative tribunals, or courts. In order to increase the efficiency of his inspections, he has begun to concentrate on a special topic or area each year, such as the method of handling juvenile delinquents.

As is typical also of the ombudsman in Sweden, many of the complaints received are without reasonable foundation, and only a small proportion require serious investigation. As a result, the staffs of the chancellor and the ombudsman are small, that of the chancellor requiring, besides an assistant chancellor, only about ten lawyers. For many years the ombudsman required only two trained lawyers, but in the 1960s his case load grew to such an extent that in 1967 a third lawyer, an expert in military law, was added to his staff, and in 1971 the legislature provided for a full-time assistant ombudsman to replace the part-time deputy ombudsman, who acted only when the ombudsman was absent.

Some indication of the nature of the cases dealt with by the ombudsman and the chancellor may be gained by comparing figures on the total number and the disposition of their cases for a single year. In 1970, for instance, the ombudsman's office handled 1098 cases, or about four per working day. Of these, 109 were initiated by the ombudsman himself, the rest being complaints. In 1029 of the cases no action was necessary: in 241 cases there were insufficient grounds for complaint, in another 528 no fault was found with the initial action either because the cases did not fall within the jurisdiction of the ombudsman (152), were pending before a tribunal (35), or for some similar reason. But there were good grounds for complaint in 69 cases. In 17 of these the officials concerned had already satisfied the complaint, but the others resulted in 49 criticisms of official action, four discipline proceedings and seven court prosecutions.

At that time the chancellor's yearly total of cases was about the same. Not counting about 50 complaints sent on to the ombudsman for investigation, his office handled about 1000 cases a year. Of these, however, only about two-thirds were complaints from the public, and about a fifth were initiated by the chancellor himself. The rest were other types of cases arising mainly from other authorities and his supervision of the public prosecutors. The fact that the chancellor initiates a much larger number of cases than the ombudsman is partly explained by the chancellor's close supervision of the courts, from which he receives full reports on all persons sentenced to fine or imprisonment. An indication of the relative importance of the chancellor's initiative is that, while complaints from the public result in four or five prosecutions a year, cases initiated by the chancellor result in 40-50. Cases requiring remedial action in the form of prosecution, discipline proceedings or criticism constitute about 20 per cent of the total, compared to about 10 per cent for the ombudsman. By 1981, the total number of cases handled by the ombudsman had risen to 2123, while the number of complaints to the chancellor had risen to 4,428.

The proportion of their cases requiring some kind of remedial action may not seem very large, but this is roughly comparable to the experience of the ombudsmen in Sweden, and again explains why the offices of the chancellor and ombudsman are able to remain small. As Professor Chapman has observed, a democracy should be ashamed of even one substantial case of injustice per year.

As with the comparable offices in Sweden, neither the chancellor nor the ombudsmam has the power to make judicial decisions involving punishment, but only to investigate and to reprimand or prosecute. But because of their power to reprimand publicly in their annual reports, and to prosecute if necessary, they exert a strong influence in preventing illegal, unjust and arbitrary actions by officials. This preventive influence is incalculable, of course, but since most of the matters with which they deal cannot, or could not otherwise, be subjected to review by the courts, there is no doubt that it is profound.

A good measure of the importance of the defenders of the law is their position relative to other senior officials. Significantly, their salaries are higher than that of any departmental official and as high as the presidents of the two supreme courts. But the latter probably have a little more prestige. For instance, one chancellor accepted an appointment as president of the supreme court and another as president of the supreme administrative court. And one ombudsman accepted an appointment to the latter court at a salary even slightly lower than his former salary (but we must keep in mind that this appointment had the advantage of permanency when compared with the ombudsman's four-year term). There seem to have been no political considerations in these appointments in the sense that they may have represented successful efforts to remove from office defenders of the law who were too zealous as watchdogs over the government. Although this is certainly a potential danger, the possibility of promoting the defenders of the law also makes it possible to "kick upstairs" those who may be inefficient or ineffective. This may become desirable even for an ombudsman, because he cannot be dismissed during his four-year term, even if the diet is dissolved and a new one elected.

The Significance of the Two Offices

To the modern efficiency expert it might appear that, since they overlap so much, the offices of chancellor and ombudsman are an unnecessary duplication. Yet it must not be forgotten that the one is an office of the executive and the other of the legislature. The Finns have been wise enough not to put all of their eggs in one basket. The chancellor's office might easily be captured by the executive if - as in recent times - the president and the prime minister should represent the same political party. It is true that the chancellor holds office for an indefinite term, but he is appointed by the president and may be dismissed or promoted by him. Moreover, his constant association with the ministers, informally as well as formally, might in time or at times, warp his better judgment. If such should be the case, the ombudsman could become a second string to the bow.

Indeed, there are good grounds for believing that in 1960 the chancellor's office was captured by the executive. When Dr. Honka, the chancellor appointed by former president Paasikivi, reached retirement age in 1960, it was generally felt among the opposition parties that, since he had carried out his duties with the independence and fearlessness that tradition demanded of the office, President Kekkonen should reappoint him for a further term. This he did not do, however, but instead appointed a man from the high court who, though he had at one time been assistant chancellor, had also been minister of justice and was generally known to be sympathetic with the party of the president and of the prime minister, the Agrarians. Partly as a result of this action, the Democratic Socialists and four other non-Communist parties nominated Honka to run as a candidate for the presidency against Kekkonen in the 1961 election, and Honka, though not at all socialist in his political views, accepted.

The situation would not have been considered so serious had the president been a relatively weak head of state as he is in many other republican systems. For then, although the chancellor might have been a "president's man," he would not necessarily have been overly sympathetic with the prime minister and his cabinet. But in Finland the office of president has always been strong, and under President Kekkonen the relations between president and prime minister became ominously like those between DeGaulle and his prime minister in France.

In view of these developments, the importance of the ombudsman as a second line of defence is clear. But it may be that his term is too short to give the office the kind of independence and strength that it deserves. Originally, the ombudsman was appointed for only one year, but in 1933 his term was extended to three years and in 1958 to four, the same length as, but not corresponding with, the term of the diet. Since he is an officer of the diet, it is of course understandable that one diet should not wish to bind its successor to an officer appointed by it. And there is some cogency to the argument that if a government should succeed in capturing both the chancellor and the ombudsman, and if a new diet could not choose a new ombudsman, a new government would have to face a chancellor and an ombudsman appointed under a previous régime, both of whom may be hostile. But on balance it appears that the long term of office is better. For a hostile chancellor and ombudsman would not create as serious a situation as ones who are too sympathetic with the executive. And if the ombudsman, too, served for a long term, it would be more difficult for a government to capture both offices, particularly if their appointments were so arranged that they retired at different times. Moreover, an ombudsman appointed for a long term would be much less subject to political influence from members of the diet in his handling of individual cases, and would become better known, and more influential and proficient as he gained experience. Much the same result could be obtained, of course, through the existence of a strong tradition that the ombudsman should be reappointed to office. But in Finland this has not been the case. During the 1920s, when appointment was annual, there were several ombudsmen, and though in the succeeding history of the office there have been a number of reappointments, this has not been the rule, with the result that the refusal to reappoint can become a weapon against the ombudsman. In 1950, for example, it was widely believed that the then ombudsman was refused reappointment because of his opposition to the Kekkonen government's handling of a railway strike.

Lessons to be Learned

From this information about the defenders of the law in Finland, what lessons may be learned for application elsewhere, especially in countries that have inherited the British parliamentary system and common law? Of course, it is never safe to assume that a particular governmental institution will work well if transplanted without adjustment to an entirely different system. But one conclusion seems clear: if countries like Finland and Sweden, which have a system of administrative courts and opportunities to appeal official decisions, find it necessary in addition to have - not one, but two - special institutions to investigate complaints of official arbitrariness, then it is all the more necessary that the common law countries should have at least one similar defender of the law.

Apparently Denmark and Norway, which, like the Commonwealth countries, do not have administrative courts in the European tradition, reached a similar conclusion when they decided to adopt the ombudsman institution. In these countries, where the courts are entirely independent of and separate from the administration, the ombudsman has not been given any control over judges or the courts. It was argued by judges and lawyers that this might interfere with the traditional independence of the judiciary. Yet this does not appear to have occurred in either Sweden or Finland, for the defenders of the law themselves are eminent jurists who are careful not to interfere with the regular judicial processes. They deal only with exceptional cases of obvious miscarriage of justice. And the number of such cases in these countries reveals that, after all, judges are only human and not infallible as our folk myths lead us to believe. If the ombudsman is not to have jurisdiction over the courts, then the courts should have their own defender of the law to investigate such cases.

A second conclusion, deriving in particular from the nature of the Finnish office of chancellor of justice, is that there is a good case for extending the powers of the defender of the law to the highest offices in the land, including cabinet ministers. It is perfectly obvious that even ministers are not above human weakness in the form of partisanship, bias, arbitrariness, self-interest and even, at times, outright corruption. One has only to think of recent cases in the Canadian provinces: in Quebec a former premier arbitrarily removed the license of a restaurant owner because he granted bail to arrested members of an unpopular religious sect; in Ontario a minister of highways was forced to resign because of scandals in his department; and in British Columbia a minister was accused of accepting a large bribe. Usually such cases are investigated and possibly prosecuted only after vigorous demands by the opposition and the appointment of a special commission or committee of investigation. But in the Commonwealth parliamentary system, where it is usual for a dominant majority party to support a dominant government and where official secrecy prevails, it is difficult for the opposition to obtain the relevant information on which to base a complaint, and easy for the government to temporize, or to appoint an investigating body that will whitewash the matter. In Finland, ordinarily the president and prime minister provide a check upon one another, and even when they are of the same political stripe, their party usually holds far less than a majority of the legislature. Majority support, especially over a long period of time, provides a fearful concentration of power in the hands of the government compared with this.

In Finland, although the chancellor may initiate a proposal for indictment of the president, and the ombudsman of a minister, neither may decide independently to proceed with prosecution. The chancellor's prosecution of the president or the ombudsman's prosecution of a minister would be undertaken only at the express direction of the diet, while the chancellor would prosecute a minister only by order of the president. Either of them, however, may initiate and independently carry through the prosecution of a member of the supreme court or of the supreme administrative court. And either of them may make recommendations (the chancellor to the president and the ombudsman to the diet), which are published in their annual reports. If the president refuses a chancellor's proposal to indict a minister, the chancellor is free to report on the case directly to the diet. Moreover, the diet could decide independently that a minister should be prosecuted, without first having received such a recommendation from the chancellor or the ombudsman. These provisions demonstrate how elaborate is the system of checks and balances contained in the Finnish constitution.

It is perhaps desirable that in Finland the defenders of the law should not have the power to proceed against a minister without the approval of either the president or legislature, but under a parliamentary system where the legislature is dominated by a government majority, one wonders whether an ombudsman should not have this power. Certainly the provision that either the chancellor or the ombudsman may proceed against a minister or other high official is a valuable safeguard, for if the chancellor has been captured by the executive or is merely weak, the ombudsman is still free to initiate and carry through a prosecution. This situation has occurred in recent Finnish history, and of course has enhanced the prestige and importance of the ombudsman relative to the chancellor. The relative importance of their offices thus varies according to circumstances and the relative strength of their personalities.

It is sometimes argued that ministers should not be inhibited by an ombudsman because of the modern need for ministerial discretion: it is difficult to draw the line between a matter of law and a matter of discretion, and in his zeal a defender of the law would be likely to infringe upon matters of discretion and policy. But this is typical of the many false fears that accompanied the proposal for an ombudsman elsewhere: the answer is that chancellors of justice and ombudsmen in Sweden and Finland have been wise enough to recognize the problem and to stick as closely as possible to matters of law - just as the judges have in common law countries. Yet elsewhere it appears that this argument has been used successfully to limit the jurisdiction of the ombudsman over ministers. More likely the real reason for this limitation is that, since cabinets control major reform legislation, cabinets elsewhere have taken advantage of their opportunity to refuse a limitation upon their own freedom of action.

Another frequent argument against an ombudsman for large countries is that to work successfully the office must be highly personalized and therefore single: the citizens must feel that they know and trust the ombudsman, and that he will give their case his personal attention, but this would be an impossibility in a populous country. Yet, Finland and Sweden do not have a single official to handle complaints against the administration. Finland has two such officers, while Sweden has a chancellor of justice plus four ombudsmen. The evidence indicates that the personal touch of a single ombudsman is less important than the independence of the office. It must be publicly known that the office is independent enough to be able to fight cases to the finish and to initiate inquiries into serious allegations of maladministration. It should not be forgotten that most of the important cases of illegality or maladministration are revealed by investigations taken on a law defender's own initiative, touched off by either his own inspections, newspaper stories or information received directly from within the civil service, the prisons, the armed services or the courts.

A related and equally illogical argument against an ombudsman for large countries is that he would be overwhelmed with work. But if this should turn out to be the case, it would be an indication of the need for a more comprehensive system of administrative appeal, with the ombudsman handling only the exceptional cases, rather than an argument for rejecting the office.

To sum up, then, it seems clear that, when the experience of Finland is added to that of Sweden, the office of parliamentary ombudsman would be an asset to any democratic country. In countries with a parliamentary system of government, the growing cabinet domination of parliament virtually demands the appointment of such an officer. He should be accountable only to parliament, should be appointed on a nonpartisan basis for a long term, and should be removable only by parliament. Moreover, his jurisdiction should extend to all administrative authorities, and to the highest officials in the land.

Footnotes - Chapter Two

1. The Profession of Government (London, 1959), ch. 12.

2. "Finland's Defenders of the Law," Canadian Public Administration IV, 3 (September 1961), and IV, 4 (December 1961), 316-325 and 412-415, and The Ombudsman in Finland: The First Fifty Years (Berkeley: Institute of Governmental Studies, 1973).

3. For much of the information on which this chapter is based, I am indebted to Dr. O. Honka, former Chancellor of Justice of Finland, and Professor P. Kastari, former Parliamentary Ombudsman, whom I interviewed in Finland.

4. Paavo Kastari, "The Constitutional Protection of Fundamental Rights in Finland," Tulane Law Review, Vol. XXXIV, p. 696.

3

THE FIRST POST-WAR ADOPTIONS

We have seen that Finland's provision for an ombudsman was a natural outgrowth of its long association with Sweden, and of its adoption of parliamentary institutions under the republican constitution of 1919. There were no further adoptions until after the second world war, when a third Nordic country, Norway, set up an ombudsman scheme for the armed services in 1952. Denmark then made provision for a general plan under its new constitution of 1953, and appointed its first ombudsman in 1955. After that, the adoptions were more rapid: West Germany provided for a military ombudsman in 1957; Norway added a general ombudsman for all civil administration in 1962; and in the same year New Zealand became the first country in the Commonwealth to adopt the plan.

Comparison with Original Systems

The general ombudsman plans adopted in Denmark, Norway, and New Zealand are modelled closely on the Swedish and Finnish originals. Although in most essentials they are the same as the originals, some significant changes were made. It is mainly the new versions, especially the one in Denmark, which have become the model for the rest of the world.

Perhaps the most significant change was that, in all three countries, the ombudsman was not given the power to supervise judges. This was partly because Denmark and Norway had no close counterpart of the chancellor of justice, and no tradition of his supervision over the courts. A second reason was that in these countries adequate supervisory and complaint machinery already existed within the court system itself. A third reason was the view that an agency of the legislature should not supervise the courts. This conventional wisdom has also prevailed in New Zealand, and, so far, elsewhere. Yet its logic is difficult to see. In Sweden the ombudsmen are non-partisan and independent of legislative influence in individual cases. They review judicial behaviour, not the content of court decisions, and do not infringe on the political independence of judges. Their cases provide numerous examples which demonstrate that judges are only human and therefore fallible. The experience of the Commission on Judicial Qualifications in California, which handles complaints against the judiciary, bears out this conclusion. [1]

A second important difference from the original systems was the confidentiality of the ombudsman's investigations. None of these countries had yet adopted the Swedish-Finnish principle that administrative documents are open to the public and the press. The amount of publicity given to a case was therefore mainly at the discretion of the ombudsman himself, and ordinarily no publicity was given until an investigation had been completed. One may question whether this degree of confidentiality was necessary. True, it would be unfair to reveal the names of officials against whom accusations had been made before the ombudsman had completed an investigation, because the accusations may be false. However, even where the Swedish-Finnish system of general administrative openness has been adopted in order to implement the democratic principle of the public's "right to know," [2] the names of officials are not ordinarily revealed at this stage.

A third significant difference in the newer schemes is that the ombudsmen have not been given the specific power to inspect or audit administrative transactions. As a result, though they do some inspections, they initiate fewer cases on their own. In Sweden a large proportion of the more serious cases arise in this way, and the ombudsmen's recommendations on them result in important administrative improvements. The Swedish ombudsmen thus act as a permanent commission on administrative procedure and efficiency. This may be the main reason why about 15 per cent of their cases result in remedial action, compared with only about 10 per cent for the newer plans.

Other differences are that in the newer plans the ombudsman was not given the power to prosecute officials, and that in Denmark and Norway he was not permitted to criticize the wisdom or content of an administrative decision but only the fairness of the procedure by which the decision was made. These differences are not of great significance, however. In the newer schemes he may still order or recommend a prosecution. In the older ones and in New Zealand, the ombudsmen rarely criticize the substance of decisions because they realize that in such matters they should not substitute their judgment for that of the responsible administrators. Since the line between the content of a decision and the way in which it is made is a thin one, the Danes have wisely given the ombudsman a chance to intervene if necessary, by using a vague word to restrict his powers. He may challenge a decision if he thinks it "unreasonable." The

Norwegian law restricts his powers a little more by saying that the decision must be "clearly unreasonable." New Zealand's law, on the other hand, may have gone too far in the other direction, by allowing him to intervene if he simply thinks a decision is "wrong."

It should also be noted that the newer plans provided for only a single ombudsman, though in Norway the general ombudsman was added to an existing plan for a military ombudsman. New Zealand later abandoned the concept of a single officer, when local government was included in 1976, and provided for three ommbudsmen, one of whom is named chief ombudsman. Since 1980, however, there have been only two ombudsmen, one of whom supervises local government.

The Plans in Operation

The first three transplanted versions of the ombudsman system seem to have worked with great success. Because they provided for a single ombudsman, their success depended very much upon the background and character of the first man appointed to the office. Highly respected lawyers with much administrative knowledge were appointed, and they were successively reappointed at the end of their four year terms. For instance, the Danish parliament chose as its first citizens' defender the man who had been the main advocate of the office at the time Denmark's new constitution was adopted - Stephan Hurwitz, an eminent professor of law. He was continually reappointed until his retirement and replacement by Lars Nielsen, former Director of Prison Administration, in 1971. Similarly, both Norway and New Zealand were pleased with their first ombudsman. In Norway, where the socialist government was defeated in 1965 after twenty years in power, the new parliament re-elected the first ombudsman for civilian affairs, Andreas Schei, to a second term. And in New Zealand, not long after the appointment of Sir Guy Powles, his position was the only senior one for which a royal commission considering civil service salaries recommended a salary increase.

During his first full year in office, Professor Hurwitz received 869 complaints. Some of these, of course, were from cranks and troublemakers, but not as many as might be expected. Of the genuine grievances, many did not fall within his jurisdiction, such as cases involving judges and the courts. They were referred to the competent authority. Other cases were not considered serious enough for detailed investigation. Professor Hurwitz and his staff of ten - including five lawyers - finally winnowed the 869 complaints down to 439 for full investigation. Each year, as the office became better known, the number of complaints increased; it is now running well over 1400 a year. But, because of the increasing sophistication of the ombudsman and his staff in knowing which cases are worthy of full investigation, the proportion investigated has declined.

Case experience with the first three transplanted systems has been surprisingly similar, and very much like that in Sweden and Finland. In proportion to population, the number and types of complaints (excepting, of course, complaints against the courts), and the number requiring remedial action, are roughly the same. All three countries have small populations, ranging from three to five million, and each ombudsman's office receives about 1,500 complaints per year. About a third of them are outside the ombudsmen's jurisdiction and most of the remainder they find unwarranted; but in about 10 per cent of the total, they find that the complaint is justified and take appropriate action to satisfy the grievance and improve the future efficiency of administration.

Before the adoption of the transplanted plans, especially in Denmark, the civil servants opposed the proposal because they feared harassment by the ombudsman and the attendant publicity. Afterward, however, they rapidly changed their views because they found that the ombudsman's rejection of unwarranted complaints enhanced the public's confidence in the civil service. They even found the ombudsman to be a valuable protection in their own complaints against superiors.

The fact that no important revisions of the newer schemes have been found necessary is a good indication that they have been working successfully. Indeed, the most significant change has been to extend the ombudsman's jurisdiction to include local government administration, as in the older systems.

Types of Cases in Denmark

The nature of the cases that the ombudsman has investigated in Denmark shows a wide variety of citizens' complaints that arise out of modern government activity, and the great need for such an office. Similar grounds for complaint arise every day in other countries but often never see the light of day. Typical examples are: the complaint that inadequate consent had been given for mental patients to undergo shock treatment and brain operations; that an elderly woman had been arrested in the middle of the night by policemen who wouldn't let her dress properly; that the authorities had unjustifiably refused to remove an acquitted complainant's photographs and fingerprints from police files. The ombudsman has also on his own intiative visited and reported on conditions in prisons and other penal institutions, and has given prisoners a chance to talk to him with no prison officials present.

Aside from cases such as these, directly involving personal liberty, there are many less serious complaints of various kinds, ranging even to the complaint of a woman passenger that a bus driver had insulted her for legitimately objecting to smoking by other passengers on a state-owned bus. The result of the ombudsman's investigation was that the authorities made the bus driver apologize, and promised to enforce the no-smoking rule.

As might be expected, many of the minor complaints involve unnecessary delay by government departments. The ombudsman took a strong line on this question and insisted that the time required to deal with cases be shortened. For example, the Danish Tax Appeal Board was criticized in the press for its leisurely operations, so the ombudsman investigated its procedure and proposed desirable changes.

Another type of case involves failure to give adequate information to the citizen - either on the current state of his case, on his right of appeal, or on the reasons for a decision. For example, a citizen complained that he could get no answer to an application for a license he had made to the customs department. The reason, it turned out, was that the department was reconsidering the rules in question and felt that it should not issue further licenses until a new policy had been decided. The citizens' defender concluded that the department should have informed the applicant of this. Similarly, he held that an applicant to the trade ministry should have been informed that the reason for the ministry's delay was that it was preparing new legislation on the subject in question.

In another case an unsuccessful applicant sent a letter to the industrial injuries directorate protesting against a decision. The directorate did not answer the letter. When a complaint was sent to the ombudsman, he held that the latter ought to have been regarded as a request for an appeal and been forwarded to the Ministry of Social Affairs, as the appellate body. In any case, the applicant should have been informed that there was a right of appeal. The ombudsman similarly criticized a tax board that decided a case to the disadvantage of an applicant without giving him a chance to argue the case.

Another procedural type of case involves the possibility of bias on the part of officials. After investigating such a case, the ombudsman recommended a change in the tax legislation to avoid the situation whereby some tax officials were members of appeal bodies hearing cases that the same officials had decided in the first place.

Cases such as these are clearly not peculiar to Denmark, and may even sound familiar to persons in other countries.

Sample Cases from New Zealand

In order to give the reader an impression of how the ombudsman operates in a country which has inherited the English parliamentary system and common law, some typical cases from New Zealand are presented below. These are quoted directly from the ombudsmen's annual reports, where each year about 100 cases, involving many departments and agencies, are reported on. Most of them strike a familiar chord in the sense that they could easily have happened anywhere.

Supervision of Police - The complainants in this case were father and son. The father held a responsible position in the community and expressed his concern regarding the manner in which his 22-year old son had been questioned by a constable. In particular he objected to certain remarks which the constable had addressed to his son, and to the fact that the interrogation was carried out in an open office where a civilian staff member of the Police Department was working within earshot.

After studying the official files, I found that the Police had justifiable grounds for questioning the son in relation to certain conduct which had aroused the suspicions of the Police, but nevertheless the remarks made by the constable and the semi-public nature of the interrogation were both open to criticism.

On representing my views to the Department, it was agreed that some admonitory action would be taken.

I informed both complainants accordingly and subsequently received a letter of thanks from the father of the young man.

Conflict of Interest - A professional photographer complained that the driver of a Government tourist car was taking advantage of the opportunities offered by the nature of his occupation to operate a secondary business as a professional photographer and vendor of scenic

34

photographs and postcards and of souvenirs. The complainant claimed that this amounted to unfair competition damaging to her own interests. On inquiry, it transpired that the complainant's husband was also a Government tourist car driver, and, as my investigation proceeded, the wife of the driver, who was the subject of the original complaint, also complained in turn of the commercial activities of the complainant's husband.

As a result of my investigation both drivers were required by the employing Department [Railways] to give identical undertakings to the effect that their commercial activities would cease, and a general instruction in similar terms was sent to all other tour drivers.

Unemployment Benefits - The complainant, who had become unemployed, alleged that officials in the local office of the Labour Department had failed properly to advise her in respect of her entitlement to unemployment benefit and as a result she had suffered financial hardship.

On taking the matter up with the Department I found that there had been some misunderstanding on both sides. This was ironed out and resulted in the Department of Labour agreeing to recommend to the Social Security Department that retrospective payment be made for the period of unemployment.

This was done and the Social Security Commission subsequently approved of a benefit being paid.

The complainant, on receipt of the approved benefit, again complained, this time alleging that the benefit was paid only for a portion of the period of her unemployment and I explained to her that a benefit is not normally granted in respect of the first seven days of a period of unemployment, and that such a period is deemed to commence after the date on which payment of wages (including holiday pay) ceases.

Deportation of Aliens - The Minister of Immigration had issued a deportation order against an illegal immigrant who had married a New Zealand girl. The wife and her father made strong appeals, on personal hardship grounds, after representations to the Minister had been unsuccessful.
Because the order was lawfully made in accordance with firm Government policy by the Minister personally, the matter was outside my jurisdiction, and I could only

suggest to the wife that if she were left in distressed circumstances as a result of the order, she should consult the local office of the Social Security Department.

Public Housing - This complaint related to the dilapidated condition of several departmental houses in a residential area. The complainant alleged that the disreputable state of the properties concerned had the effect of devaluing other properties in the locality.

The Department [of Railways] informed me that the houses had been purchased in connection with land acquisition for railway purposes and had not been specially acquired for staff housing. They were old and rundown when purchased and had there not been an acute shortage of housing would have been demolished. Most of the houses were let on a "restricted" tenancy basis, the occupants being responsible for maintenance.

Owing to the fact that the houses would have to be removed within a few years to make way for a new railway, the Department felt that expenditure in renovation was not really warranted, but now agreed to do some minor repairs and external painting and to inform the tenants of their responsibilities in keeping the properties clean and tidy so that a reasonable standard of appearance would now be attained.

I informed the complainant accordingly.

Delayed Payment - The complainant had had difficulty in obtaining payment of a substantial amount of arrears of remuneration which he believed he had been promised by the [Maritime] Department. The amount was urgently needed to meet a family commitment. I asked the Head Office to look into the matter, and this resulted in arrangements for payment being made immediately.

Customs - The complainant was the father of a New Zealander serving at an overseas station of the Royal Air Force. In anticipation of leave in New Zealand in a few month's time, and of an expected reposting, the son sent several crates of his personal effects to his father, who was, however, informed by the Customs agents that the Customs would not permit him to collect the crates, and that in the meantime he would be required to pay 6s. per week storage.

The Customs Department explained that the agents had endeavoured to clear the crates under the tariff concession relating to passenger's baggage and effects, and in the meantime warehoused the goods pending the arrival of their owner.

As it was clear that the difficulties were due to lack of understanding and proper instructions as between the complainant, his son, and the Customs agent, the Collector of Customs at Auckland was asked to explain to the complainant precisely how the goods could be cleared (including the amount of deposit required against possible duty liability) pending his son's arrival. The complainant complied and secured delivery of the crates.

Voting Rights - An adult citizen of New Zealand had failed to enrol as an elector on attaining the age of 21 and was absent from his electorate during each of the next two Parliamentary elections.

He voted each time as an absentee voter, and did not become aware that his votes were invalid until he made inquiries in his own electorate after the rolls for the next election had closed. He then found that as he had never been on the roll, his previous votes must have been treated as invalid, and that he would not be able to vote in the current elections. He maintained that any voter whose vote was classed as invalid should be informed of the reason, so that he could correct the fault before the ensuing elections.

My inquiries showed that it was a normal and approved departmental practice for Registrars of Electors to take action to enroll those persons who had cast special votes but whose names did not appear on current electoral rolls. It seemed that the instructions on this point had not been followed on either of the occasions on which the complainant had cast a special vote. Accordingly the attention of all Returning Officers and Registrars was again especially drawn to the instructions by the Chief Electoral Officer, and the Department [of Justice] stated that consideration would be given to the desirability of amending the Electoral Regulations to provide that a special voter whose vote had been disallowed should be informed of the reason.

Public Employee - The complainant, who was over 65 years of age, had been employed on the temporary staff of the Public Service for almost 10 years. Although younger employees received 15 days leave after five years of service, he was granted 10 days only and his application for 15 days had been declined.

When I took the matter up, the State Services Commission conceded that the complainant was entitled to 15 days under the existing legislation relating to annual leave, and I advised the complainant accordingly.

The case drew to the Commission's attention a discrepancy between its Instructions Manual regarding annual leave and the legislative rulings under which those instructions were issued.

What is striking in these cases is the role of the ombudsman in humanizing administration. He accomplishes this by acting as a conduit of communication both between the citizen and government and among civil servants and departments. Not only are grievances remedied, but the likelihood of their reoccurrence is lessened.

Footnotes - Chapter Three

1. See Stanley V. Anderson, ed., Ombudsmen for American Government?, op. cit., ch. 5.

2. See my "The Right to Government Information in Democracies," International Review of Administrative Sciences 1 (1982), 59-69 (a revision of an address to the Symposium on Freedom of Information organized by the Asahi newspaper, Tokyo, May 20, 1981).

4

WEST GERMANY'S MILITARY OMBUDSMAN

The West German magazine called Quick, the equivalent of Life in the United States, in its issue of June 21, 1964, featured an explanation of Die Beatles of why they were not going to visit Germany and, more sensationally, the first of three articles criticizing the West German army. The story said the army was becoming a state within a state and was in danger of recapturing the authoritarian spirit of the Prussian and Nazi armies. This, the article continued, was in direct violation of the democratic principles that are supposed to be basic to the new German army. The story also added to the list of shocking cases of army authoritarianism that had been getting widespread publicity in West Germany in recent months.

In one such case, a young noncommissioned officer became so angry with a recruit who couldn't shoot a rifle properly, that he shot forty-eight perfect shots himself and then, to drive the lesson home, struck the recruit forty-eight times. In another case, some officers tried to toughen 150 recruits by rounding them up on the main floor of a barracks building and exposing them to tear gas and blank machine-gun fire. In still another, a paratroop recruit, who was supposed to be standing at attention, turned his head to watch a girl go by; his punishment was a large number of pushups - above the cutting edge of an army knife. But the event that forced most of these revelations was a training march for some very raw recruits. It was a hot day, the march was ten miles long, and one boy died from exhaustion.

The Quick articles caused a public furor. Part of the controversy was due to the authority and personality of their author, Vice-Admiral Hellmuth Heye. He could not be brushed off by the Erhard government as a cranky old publicity seeking soldier. Heye was Germany's military ombudsman, or Parliamentary Commissioner for Military Affairs - a special official who had been appointed by parliament to oversee the conduct of the armed forces.

I happened to be in Bonn just as this story broke, and I had a direct interest in the affair. I had been studying the office of ombudsman in Scandinavia and New Zealand and had recently finished editing my book of essays on the application of the idea to the English-speaking world. I was anxious to gain a firsthand knowledge of the military ombudsman in West Germany, and, thanks to Quick, the press was full of stories about Vice-Admiral Heye, his job and his accusations. Mixed in with these was a controversy about the propriety of parliament's ombudsman writing such an article for a popular magazine, instead of reporting only to parliament. He had just been called before Dr. Gerstenmaier, President of the Bundestag (the lower house of the German parliament), who had publicly criticized him for his action at a press conference, and he and his chief assistant were asked to appear before a parliamentary committee.

The next stage in the publicity was a thirteen page spread of stories in the June 24th issue of Der Spiegel news magazine, with Vice-Admiral Heye's picture featured on the front page. Der Spiegel is the West German equivalent of Time, and in fact is closely patterned on Time, except that it considers itself the self-appointed watchdog of the government and of German democracy. Readers may recall the "Der Spiegel Affair" a year or so before this. The editors of Der Spiegel were accused by former Minister of Defense Strauss of publishing information that was supposedly secret, and one of the editors was imprisoned. The storm raised over this affair caused the resignation of the Minister and contributed to Chancellor Adenauer's resignation. It is not surprising that Der Spiegel decided to feature the military ombudsman's accusations and actions in a sympathetic light. Its spread of stories included a history of the ombudsman's office, a human-interest story on Heye himself, part of his report to parliament, and an interview with a senior official of the defence department containing his replies to the ombudsman's accusations.

History of the Office

Perhaps the most interesting feature of the whole Heye affair is that such an extensive controversy about the principles of army organization in a democracy would never have been raised if there had been no military ombudsman. The office was provided for when the new German army was created in 1956, and was designed to maintain parliamentary control over the military and to ensure that the army would develop according to the new democratic spirit of the citizen in uniform. It was patterned after the military ombudsman in Sweden, and was first proposed in West Germany by a member of the Socialists and then grudgingly approved by the Christian Democratic Union, the governing party, in order to gain the support of the Socialists for the constitutional amendment necessary to re-establish the army. After this amendment was passed in 1956, it was a full year before the amendment and law establishing the Parliamentary Commissioner for Military Affairs went through. Another year and a half passed before a suitable man could be found, so the office did not go into actual operation until 1959.

Under the constitution this special officer of parliament is given power to oversee the conduct of the armed forces and to protect the rights of soldiers. One of the interesting features of the office - copied from the similar office in Sweden - is that he has power to receive complaints directly from soldiers at the lowest level about the way in which they have been treated by their superior officers. After receiving such complaints he has the right to inquire into them at any level of the armed forces or defence department, and to see any relevant files or documents. On his own he can visit all troops, staffs and administrative agencies of the armed forces if there is evidence of violating a soldier's rights. He must send reports to parliament at least once each year about his activities and the complaints that he has received, and he may make recommendations for improving the conditions he has found.

The first military ombudsman to be appointed by parliament was a former lieutenant-general, Helmuth von Grolman. His first report to parliament in 1960 was somewhat critical of army conditions. Some opponents of the office argued that he had been too critical, and proposed that either the new office should be abolished or the competence of the ombudsman should be narrowed. His second report in 1961 was less critical. In July of that year he was forced to resign because of a scandal in his private life.

It was not until the fall of 1961 that Helmuth Heye was appointed. His first report was relatively non-controversial but his second report was more critical. It was because not enough attention was paid to this report by members of parliament and the press that Ombudsman Heye felt justified in giving wide publicity to the conclusions of his third report. His opponents, however, pointed out that this report was presented to parliament only one week before his first article appeared in Quick. It was obvious, they said, that he had no intention of giving the members of parliament a chance to review the accusations and recommendations made in his report before he gave them such wide publicity. So the ombudsman's action in publishing the article became a kind of red herring which was used by the government, the defence department and others to sidetrack the main issue: "Was the German army going back to its old authoritarian ways?" The independence of the ombudsman's office and its power to investigate conditions at the lowest levels suggest that there must have been a good deal of truth in Heye's accusations.

This is further supported by the character of Heye himself. During the second world war, he had commanded a small élite troop of submarine and torpedo commandos. In the 1930's he had been bold enough to state in a memorandum to his supreme commander that Nazi Germany was very similar to the totalitarian regime in communist Russia. He had also warned that the plans Hitler was demanding from his general staff for an attack on Czechoslovakia and Poland would lead eventually to a world war which could end only in disaster for Germany, and that it was neither a just nor a necessary war. And he had criticized strongly the policies that had been instituted by the Nazis for the build-up and training of the armed forces. Even at that early stage he had already suggested that it was essential to have people who could think for themselves if they were to handle modern arms, rather than a body of obedient automatons.

After the war he became a member of the Christian Democratic Union, the major party, and in 1953 he was elected to parliament where he held a seat until 1961 when he was defeated by a candidate of the Socialist party, the SPD. Even during that period he was not always a comfortable colleague for the other members of the CDU. For instance, in 1953, in the presence of Chancellor Adenauer, he criticized the plans of the CDU for the new army in such scathing terms that Adenauer left the room in anger. Partly because of the independent stand he frequently took with his own party, when he was appointed military ombudsman in 1961 the SPD, which is the main opposition party, also approved his appointment.

Results of the Heye Affair

Vice-Admiral Heye's history demonstrates his independence of mind, and I suspect that he was prepared for the storm that his accusations, and his unprecedented action in publishing them in a popular magazine, would create. He justified his action by stating that the statements made in his article were based on his annual report to parliament, and that his comments in his annual report would not have had sufficient impact if he had not done this. Certainly, his previous report to parliament had caused very little stir, whereas his popular articles created a great debate in the whole country over what principles and procedures should be applied in a modern democratic army. Discussions of this problem were stimulated not only in parliament and in the popular press but also within the army itself, from the lowest to the highest levels. It is not an easy problem to solve in any democratic country because of the inherently hierarchical nature of army authority. Although West Germany had made a genuine attempt to set up its army on a new and democratic basis, one of the main difficulties was the absence of middle-ranking and senior officers in the 40-60 age group who understood and were sympathetic with the new principles being applied. As a result, West Germany had to rely in its upper echelons on some of the older officers from the Nazi army. Even within the army, however, the great majority of senior officers agreed with Heye's view that there was a danger of the early enthusiasm for a citizen's army losing its force, of the army becoming socially separated from the rest of society, and of authoritarianism creeping in.

There is no doubt that the military ombudsman's unusual action in this instance had desirable results. It forced parliament and especially the government to re-examine their policies regarding the army. Significantly, a few days after the article appeared, the government announced the appointment, as Inspector-General of the Armed Forces, of General Maizière, an enthusiastic defender of the principle of an army of citizens in uniform. He was also one of the original drafters of the army's so-called "principles of internal guidance" - a set of modern principles intended to define the role of the armed forces in society and the conduct of officers in relation to the men. The ombudsman's stand probably also helped to strengthen parliament in relation to a too-powerful executive. The fact that he could force such an important debate to take place was a significant mark of democratic health in West Germany.

The seriousness of Heye's charges should not be exaggerated. It is easy for outsiders to be persuaded that West Germany's army is no different from the old Nazi or Prussian armies. But one should not forget that a genuine attempt was made in 1956 to found an army on democratic lines. It was a new army under a new constitution and a new set of principles. The discussions in West Germany about the principles and attitudes that should guide officers in a democratic army reflect a genuine concern about the nature of military life. The ombudsman's accusations were in themselves a spectacular demonstration of this concern.

The Value of a Military Ombudsman

There are good grounds for arguing that provision for a military ombudsman in West Germany and the controversy he raised demonstrate a healthier state of affairs than in many other democratic countries, where the authoritarian nature of the armed services is largely ignored. How to ensure civilian control of the military and how to preserve the rights of the citizen when he becomes a soldier are difficult problems to solve in any country, and have become particularly pressing with the postwar growth of modern armies. After all, cases of military cruelty or arbitrary authority are not unheard of in other democracies, including Britain, Canada and the United States. In countries which do not have an ombudsman, however, such cases are not easily brought to light. The creation of the office of military ombudsman is a significant step toward solving these problems.

A serious difficulty with the necessarily hierarchical and authoritarian organization of the armed services is that the man at the bottom of the "totem pole" has no easy way to make his complaints known. He is likely to be subjected to recriminations from above if he attempts to bypass "the normal channels." The office of military ombudsman has the advantage of providing an independent authority to which he may turn. Aside from the important function of being able to raise a major issue of policy such as that raised by Heye, the office can be invaluable in investigating and settling complaints of injustice and unfair treatment by superior officers. In 1980, for example, West Germany's military ombudsman received nearly 7,000 petitions and complaints of various kinds, many of which turned out to be justified. In case the German army is thought to be unusual in this respect, it should be noted that the special military ombudsman before 1968 in Sweden handled about 650 cases a year, while the one in Norway handles about 300. These numbers are roughly proportional to the sizes of the armies in the respective countries.

We should therefore ask whether Scandinavia and West Germany have not developed an important new institution for helping to keep the army under control and from becoming internally too authoritarian. The idea of an ombudsman for civilian affairs has been widely discussed in many countries, but not much stress has been laid on the special need for complaint machinery for the armed services. This could be provided either by extending the jurisdiction of civilian ombudsmen to the armed services, as in Sweden, Finland, Denmark and New Zealand, or by creating a special ombudsman for the services, as in Germany, Norway, and more recently Israel. The need for such machinery everywhere is shown by the fact that Israel's military complaints commissioner, established in 1972, receives about 10,000 complaints a year.

PART TWO:
THE NEED FOR
OMBUDSMEN ELSEWHERE

5

THE INADEQUACY OF
EXISTING MACHINERY

The reason for the widespread interest in the ombudsman type of institution is not far to seek: there is a need for additional protection against administrative arbitrariness in the modern democratic state. All democratic countries in the twentieth century have experienced a shift from the laissez-faire to the positive state. The accompanying tremendous growth in the range and complexity of government activities has brought with it the need to grant increasing powers of discretion to the executive side of government. As one of Britain's great constitutional lawyers, A.V. Dicey, has warned, "Wherever there is discretion, there is room for arbitrariness." In other words, it is quite possible nowadays for a citizen's rights to be accidentally crushed by the vast juggernaut of the government's administrative machine. In this age of the welfare state, thousands of administrative decisions are made each year, many of them by minor officials, which affect the lives of every citizen. If some of these decisions are arbitrary or unjustified, there is no easy way for the ordinary citizen to gain redress. In the preface to the British Whyatt Report, Lord Shawcross expressed the situation in these words:

> The general standards of administration in this country are high, probably indeed higher than in any other. But with the existence of a great bureaucracy there are inevitably occasions, not insignificant in number, when through error or indifference, injustice is done - or appears to be done. The man of substance can deal with these situations. He is near to the establishment; he enjoys the status or possesses the influence which will ensure him the ear of those in authority. He can afford to pursue such legal remedies as may be available. He knows his way around. But too often the little man, the ordinary humble citizen, is incapable of asserting himself...The little man has become too used to being pushed around; it rarely occurs to him that there is any appeal from what "they" have decided. And as this Report shows, too often in fact there is not. [1]

In the past the courts were the bulwark of individuals' rights. But the ordinary courts have lost their flexibility and are no longer an effective instrument for remedying the wrongs of modern administrative action. The courts are too costly, cumbersome and slow, and in the English-speaking world the extent of their power of review is not at all clear, though certainly severely limited. Generally, they will review a decision only on a question of legality and refuse to review its content, wisdom or even reasonableness. For these reasons, in most common-law countries special administrative appeal bodies have been created, to which an aggrieved citizen may take his case. But these bodies cover only a small portion of the total field of administrative action, and the vast majority of administrative decisions carry no formal right of appeal.

The situation is better, of course, in those European countries that have developed a comprehensive system of administrative courts, where appeal is easy and cheap. But administrative courts can be imperfect. Many of them are cumbersome and slow, so that the delay in deciding cases results in a denial of justice. It is significant that though Sweden and Finland have administrative courts, ombudsmen have also been found necessary to supervise administrative action.

The right to complain to one's member in the legislature does not meet the problem. Citizens often do not know of this avenue of appeal, and it is unsuitable anyway. They are likely to feel that their member is not impartial because of his party affiliation. Though the legislature is the traditional body in which complaints and grievances about the actions of administrators are aired, it is seriously limited in what it can do. Members are often heavily loaded with other kinds of problems and requests from their constituents. Since investigating complaints is so time-consuming, this tends to take their time away from other important functions, such as considering policy and legislation, and keeping up with events as a background for dealing with important issues. Far from reducing their importance, an ombudsman would give them time to play a more important role in law-making. True, the reduced contacts with their constituents may lessen their chances of re-election. But sitting members already have too much of an advantage over other candidates, and through their help to constituents are likely to be re-elected even if they are poor representatives and law-makers. Anyway, they would still have many contacts with constituents regarding other personal and policy matters.

In countries with a parliamentary system of government, especially where the government has been supported by a majority party for many years, the executive tends to dominate parliament and to maintain a tradition of administrative secrecy. Hence it is difficult to bring cases of maladministration to light. It is impossible for an individual citizen, or even a member of parliament, to find out exactly what went on. In some cases it is even difficult for the citizen to establish a <u>prima facie</u> case that there is suspicion of an abuse, because he cannot get at enough facts to establish this. The member's usual method of dealing with a complaint is to send an inquiry to the department concerned. Naturally the department is likely to put the best light on its own case, and the member has no impartial source of information. If he is dissatisfied with the department's reply, all he can do is ask a question of the minister in parliament. Even though the minister may have had nothing to do with the original decision, he will naturally consider himself a party to his department's decision and will defend it as his own.

About the only further recourse is for the member, still with inadequate information, to debate the complaint in parliament - in which case it will turn into a political battle with the dice loaded in favour of the minister. If the member happens to be sufficiently interested and belongs to the opposition, he might use a suspected case of maladministration as a device for embarrassing the government and might even press for an investigation. The opposition party can of course demand a formal inquiry, but an inquiry is costly and cumbersome, and is accepted by a government only after enough public outcry has been raised. Clearly it is not an adequate device for remedying the average minor administrative wrong done to the little man. The celebrated British Crichel Down case in 1954 - in which a landowner was a victim of the bungling of bureaucrats in the Ministry of Agriculture, and upset their rulings only after years of effort - proved that if a citizen is to have his case investigated by traditional means, he must be rich, well educated and persistent.

Even in countries where there is a separation of powers or a multi-party situation, where the executive is not quite so dominant, there is usually no machinery in the legislature for handling administrative complaints, with the power to get at the facts, impartially sift the evidence and, where an injustice is found, propose a suitable remedy. In some countries the legislature has a petitions committee for such complaints, but it is too inaccessible, cumbersome and slow for minor complaints, and potential complainants may suspect it of being partisan. Hence, petitions committees receive a very small number of complaints compared with ombudsmen.

Advantages of an Ombudsman

In short, in most democratic countries our traditional devices for protecting the rights of average citizens against administrative arbitrariness are inadequate, if not actually defective. Because of the shortcomings of these devices, we may conclude that the office of ombudman has a number of desirable characteristics which argue for its adoption. In the words of the Whyatt Report regarding Sweden (p. 52):

> First, there is the principle of impartial investigation. If a citizen makes a complaint against the conduct of a civil servant, the matter is investigated and reported upon by the ombudsman, who is an impartial authority entirely independent of the administration. Secondly, the impartial authority acts on behalf of parliament although he is also protecting the interests of the individual complainant. Thirdly, the investigation is conducted openly...Fourthly, the method of submitting complaints and the investigation of complaints is very informal.

And one might add that, since the great weapon of the ombudsman is criticism, he does not interfere with day-to-day administration. Unlike appeal bodies, he does not substitute his judgment for that of the official, nor does he, like the courts, quash decisions.

Another great advantage of the ombudsman is his ability to get at the facts in the hundreds of minor cases where a public inquiry or court case would be too elaborate, formal and costly. Under the general rules of administrative access in Sweden and Finland, the ombudsman's investigations there are conducted openly. Elsewhere the ombudsman only has the power to get at the facts himself, but he can reveal them at the conclusion of his investigation if he thinks it necessary. Those who are afraid of having administrative documents open to public inspection should at least be willing to grant to an officer of parliament the right of access to information for the purpose of investigating suspected cases of injustice. In countries which continue to maintain their traditional rules of administrative secrecy, an ombudsman would be a desirable step toward freer public access to information about administrative activities.

Finally, people need to know that there is some impartial authority willing to act on their behalf. Psychologically they need a "wailing wall"; they need to have some outlet to which they can go with their complaints. As a result of my writings about the ombudsman, I have myself received over the years a large number of administrative cases from complaining citizens, many of whom revealed a deep feeling of resentment because they had been unable to find an impartial authority to investigate the grievance. An unsatisfied complaint may rankle in a person's mind for years. I have received complaints that originated thirty years earlier. If there had been some source to which a complainant could have gone with the assurance of impartiality in the investigation of his case, even if he were wrong in thinking he had been treated unfairly, this would have satisfied him, and he would not have gone on worrying about it for thirty years. Few things cause so much resentment in a person as the feeling that he has not been treated fairly, or even that he may not have been treated fairly. A large part of the ombudsman's job is to satisfy complainants, through the impartiality of his investigations, that they have been treated fairly. This aspect of his work, though not revealed by statistics on the number of complaints found to be justified, is extremely important.

1. Justice [British Section of the International Commission of Jurists], The Citizen and the Administration: The Redress of Grievances - A Report, Sir John Whyatt, Director of Research (London: Stevens, 1961), XIII. This report, which proposed a parliamentary commissioner for Britain, is commonly (and hereafter) called the Whyatt Report.

6.

THE TRANSFERABILITY
OF THE OMBUDSMAN PLAN

Let us now consider some of the arguments that have been raised against transplanting the ombudsman plan. One reason the English-speaking world took so little interest in the institution before it was adopted in Denmark is that nothing was known about the Finnish plan, and not much more about the Swedish one. Of the Swedish scheme it was argued that the systems of government and law in Sweden were so different from elsewhere that the scheme could not be successfully transferred. Sweden has, in addition to the ombudsman, a system of administrative appeal courts, and a unique tradition of publicity whereby the press and the citizens may have access to departmental files at any time. More important, Sweden has an administrative system radically different from most others: Swedish departments resemble public corporations in their independence, and are not subject to detailed day-to-day control by the ministers responsible to parliament. Because of these differences, it was said that the scheme would not work elsewhere. However, its successful adoption in Denmark exploded these claims. The systems of law and cabinet government in this country resembled those of the Commonwealth much more closely; it had neither a system of administrative courts, nor a strong tradition of administrative publicity, but it did have a system of ministerial responsibility for administration characteristic of parliamentary government elsewhere.

Too much has been made of the dangers of an ombudsman's publicity, in any case. Even in Sweden there are laws against revealing state secrets or information that would be injurious to private persons or commercial firms. The names of complainants and officials involved in cases are not ordinarily revealed, and the amount of publicity given to cases is partly at the discretion of the ombudsman and is voluntarily controlled by the press. In the nature of things no publicity is given to minor cases of no news interest, and of course important cases should be discussed publicly.

A closely related argument against transplanting the office was that, in view of the ombudsmen's revelations of maladministration in the Nordic countries, the need for a check on officialdom must be greater there than elsewhere.

55

The Nordic countries, however, are among the best-governed democracies in the world. The standards of their public services are extremely high, and their provisions for appeal of administrative decisions are certainly more ample than in the English-speaking countries. In adopting the ombudsman system, Denmark and Norway have simply recognized that in the age of the welfare state, traditional controls are not good enough. As the chairman of the Norwegian Committee on Administrative Procedure expressed it:

> [Our] recommendations are not based upon any assumption or allegation on the part of the Committee that the Norwegian administrative system is a bad one or that the civil servants are incompetent. The Committee states, on the contrary, that our administration may bear comparison with any other system of administration. This is also true of the guarantees and safeguards. The reasons behind the proposals to strengthen the means of control are much more far-reaching and go deeper. They have their origin in the characteristic development of the modern welfare state. It seems unavoidable at the stage of economic and technical development which, regardless of politics, has been achieved in all modern societies, that ever larger and broader powers shall be bestowed upon the administrative authorities...This is the background against which the Norwegian proposals - and the many efforts in other countries to introduce reforms in the same field - must be considered.[1]

Curiously, the opposite argument has also been raised - that the need is greater in the English-speaking countries, and is in fact so great that an ombudsman would be overwhelmed with complaints. The Times warned (January 13, 1960) that in a large country like Britain the office might burgeon into something like the Chinese Control Yuan during the Han dynasty (206 B.C. - A.D. 220), which became a parallel branch of government constantly looking over the shoulder of the harried official. Instead of a public watchdog over the official's acts, the ombudsman might become a bloodhound sniffing after his every decision. But as the Economist replied (January 31, 1960), this argument is to stand logic on its head. It is tantamount to saying that because the demand would be overwhelming the need should not be met at all. In any case, the fear is false. The ombudsman performs his task with only a few legal officers and office assistants, and he is certainly no super-administrator with power to substitute his judgment for that of other officials. In fact, he rarely comments on the content of a discretionary decision but rather on the way in which the decision has been made, to ensure its legality and fairness.

That the bloodhound theory arises from a false fear is shown by the reversal in the attitude of civil servants in Denmark. Before the scheme was introduced they opposed it, but after its adoption they soon realized that the office was an aid rather than a hindrance. For in nine cases out of ten the ombudsman vindicated their decisions and hence increased public confidence in the civil service. The scheme also shifted much of the task of handling the public's complaints from the civil service to the ombudsman. And minor officials soon found that the ombudsman was an ally in their own dealings with arbitrary superiors. It is true, of course, that in the absence of a comprehensive system of administrative appeals, the work of an ombudsman would be greater, but this problem must be attacked at its source, by creating more opportunities for appeal.

It is frequently argued that to be the little man's defender the ombudsman's office must be a highly personal one, while in large countries the size of the office would cause it to lose this personal touch. This argument has also been inverted: it is said that the office to too personal, too dependent upon one man's integrity, understanding and daily time; and that the nature of the office demands for its success a virtual impossibility - finding exactly the right man for the job, in particular one who combines a profound knowledge of the law with wide experience in various types of administration. These arguments, too, can be easily challenged. In the first place, there has been a lot of sentimental twaddle about the ombudsman's personal touch. The principle of impartiality is far more important than the personal touch. Certainly citizens need to know that there is an independent authority to which they can turn for an impartial investigation, but this objective can be achieved without the paternalism inherent in a personalized office. Moreover, there are good grounds for the view that important and complex cases of a judicial nature should not be decided by a single person. (In fact, they are not so decided under the ombudsman scheme. Although the ombudsman deals with all important cases personally, naturally he and his expert staff discuss all such cases before he reaches a final conclusion, so that in effect they work as a group.) The old adage applied to the higher courts that two heads are better than one also applies here. For this reason I would recommend for populous countries a commission of three or more members, which might be called the Ombudsman (or Administrative Complaints) Commission. Commissioners would decide minor cases individually but important cases together. Each could specialize in a particular area or type of administration. The commission could include a judge and an experienced administrator (and perhaps also a representative of the public). In this way the proposal bypasses the argument that it is virtually impossible to find in a single man the qualities demanded by the office.

Having seen that most of the arguments that have been raised against transplanting the ombudsman scheme may be effectively demolished, we should at the same time keep in mind that it cannot be a panacea. Many people regard "Ombudsman" as a kind of magic word that will cure all administrative ills. But the age-old problem of the relation between the state and the individual is far too complex to be solved by one simple scheme. We need a whole variety of controls over administrative action, and the ombudsman scheme must be accompanied by a number of other reforms that are needed to plug the gaps in our system of control. Otherwise, the scheme may fail because we are trying to make it do too much. We must remember that in the Nordic countries and New Zealand, the scheme only supplements a battery of other effective controls, and that New Zealand added the plan to an already existing parliamentary grievance system, the petitions committee.

On the other hand, the danger in setting up a network of controls is that, if the administration is surrounded with too many controls, it will be unable to move. This is the danger in extending court review too far or in judicializing the administrative process too much. The United States has already gone too far in this direction, and recent British changes and proposals seem to point to the same danger. What we need is a fence along the administrative road, not a gate across it. The great virtue of the ombudsman scheme is that its weapons are publicity and persuasion rather than cumbersome controls; it is in the category of the fence rather than the gate.

Footnotes - Chapter Six

1. Terje Wold, "The Norwegian Parliament's Commissioner for the Civil Administration," Journal of the International Commission of Jurists, II, 2 (Winter, 1959; Spring-Summer, 1960), 24.

7.

APPLICABILITY TO DIFFERING
LEGAL SYSTEMS

As the evidence already presented shows, the Nordic countries and New Zealand are confident that they have developed
a worthwhile institution. To the people in other democratic
countries who are considering the desirability of its adoption, the important questions are these: Is it really needed
in our country? How serious are the objections that may be
raised against its adoption? Could the institution be adjusted to fit our circumstances and, if so, what adjustments
would be needed?   The answers to these questions will of
course vary somewhat from one country to another according
to the type of constitutional and legal system that each
possesses. One cannot hope to consider the detailed answers
that would have to be developed for each country in turn.
This is a job for those who have an intimate knowledge of
the inner workings of their own particular political system.
However, the countries of the western world, upon which most
other democracies have based their institutions, can be div-
ided into three types of constitutional and legal systems,
each of which has important characteristics in common.   And
in trying to answer the above questions, general statements
can be made about each type.

    First are the countries of western Europe that have a
highly developed system of administrative courts, such as
France, Italy, Germany and Austria. A common initial reaction of persons from these countries is to say that an ombudsman is not needed because administrative courts do the
job instead, and, anyway, it could not be fitted into the
administrative court system. A reply, however, is that the
job of administrative courts is not the same as that of the
ombudsman. He relies upon criticism and publicity rather
than the quashing of decisions, and is an agent of parliament rather than of the executive. Administrative courts
suffer - though admittedly to a lesser extent - from the
same shortcomings as ordinary courts in that they can be
slow, costly, cumbersome, complex, frightening to the average citizen, and limited in their power to review the merits
of decisions. Also, the highly-regarded system of administrative courts in France cannot be taken as typical. In some
other European countries the administrative courts are weak,
seriously limited in their powers, and subject to the influence of the executive. The parallel existence of a supreme

administrative court and ombudsmen in Sweden does not constitute an unnecessary overlapping or duplication of functions. An ombudsman scheme and administrative courts are so
different in function that the former need not be conceived
of as an alternative to, or as part of, the administrative
courts. It would be an additional, separate institution
fulfilling a different need. If it is regarded in this
light, the standard objections become irrelevant.

Turning now to countries that have inherited the common
law and do not have comprehensive administrative courts,
there is an important distinction between the many that have
copied the British cabinet system of government, with a
union of executive and legislative powers, and those, like
the United States and the Philippines, that have adopted a
separation of powers. Regarding the latter countries, the
deficiencies in their present legal systems seem to be much
the same as in other common-law countries, and speak in favour of an ombudsman scheme. However, because of the separation of powers and the traditional struggle between the executive and legislature, it may be objected that an ombudsman would be regarded with suspicion by the executive departments as a biased agent of Congress. The executive has
control over administrative documents and might not be prepared to give him sufficient access to information. Because
of the highly politicized nature of the presidency and of
the top administrative posts, an ombudsman would be likely
to be caught up in partisan politics. And because of the
highly decentralized nature of the political system, pressure groups are strong, and he might be swayed by them in
his decisions. It is also said that the separation of powers
enhances the role of the Congressman as an agent of his
constituents and that an ombudsman might undesirably reduce
the importance of this role. How valid these objections are
I am not in a position to say with assurance. But it is significant that a number of knowledgeable persons in the United States have come to doubt their validity and are willing
to experiment with the ombudsman institution at either the
federal, state or local levels of government.

Some of the problems raised by the separation of powers
might be overcome by creating a plural ombudsman - a complaints commission, whose members would be appointed jointly
by the executive and Congress. This could perhaps be a body
of three, with one member appointed by the President, one by
the Senate and one by the House of Representatives. The experience of the French Conseil d'Etat attests to the fact
that such a body need not be exclusively an agent of the
legislature as long as it is made sufficiently independent
of the executive. Its effectiveness would lie not so much

in its direct relationship to the legislature as in its easy accessibility to the citizens, its power to investigate, the reasonableness of its opinions on cases, and its ability to bring them to the attention of the public.

Whatever may be the need for ombudsmen in the United States, it is even greater in the Commonwealth and similar royalist countries. These countries are steeped in monarchical tradition and its undesirable implications for bureaucracy. They have not yet succeeded in throwing off the old legal theory that civil servants are servants of the King (or Emperor) rather than of the public and that the King can do no wrong. Therefore, through what one might call 'virtue by association,' civil servants can never - well, hardly ever - do wrong. Formerly officials acted on behalf of the King, and the old hierarchical myth would even have us believe that when they acted it was really the King who was acting. Hence they had to remain anonymous and their action secret. These ideas are obviously out of tune with modern democratic government, and we must ask ourselves whether the reasons we now give to defend anonymity and secrecy are not mere rationalizations, whether in reality these characteristics of bureaucracy in the Commonwealth and other countries are not preserved mainly for the convenience of the government in power. They place serious difficulties in the way of the public's legitimate access to information, its 'right to know,' in a democracy.

Clearly, the royalist tradition has carried with it legal assumptions about the 'rightness' of executive action and the superiority of the state that have made it difficult for the citizens to secure legitimate redress. Until recent years in Commonwealth countries one could not sue a government agency without the Crown's permission, and damages were paid by the Crown only as an act of grace. Even yet in some of these countries, the courts are powerless to order the production of official documents because of the doctrine of Crown privilege, and procedures for the Crown's expropriation of private property are often arbitrary. Undesirable aspects of executive power such as these have been preserved because parliament only gradually came to control the executive and because the executive still introduces most of the laws and through its majority still manages to dominate parliament. Governments have been quite willing to preserve and use prerogative powers that they find convenient, and in legislation to grant themselves or their agents extensive delegated powers.

The previous strength of the royal power has also led the courts to inherit a tradition of no fetters on executive discretion and of reticence about reviewing administrative action. This tradition has been preserved in recent times by the convenient assumption that it is the job of parliament to control the administration and that therefore any complaint about administrative action, other than its clear illegality, should be left for parliament to deal with. The courts have only hesitantly entered the arena by marking out a vague area of so-called 'judicial or quasi-judicial' administrative action for review, and the legal procedures used for bringing administrative cases before the courts are hopelessly archaic and complex in most Commonwealth countries. Because of parliament's inability to cope with the situation, our naive faith in the doctrine of ministerial responsibility has often resulted in something dangerously close to administrative irresponsibility. An ombudsman scheme would therefore be a healthy step in the direction of a better balance between the rights of the citizen and the power of the Crown.

In his essay in The Ombudsman, Professor Abel has pointed to a number of the common characteristics of the Commonwealth parliamentary systems with which an ombudsman would have to make his peace. [1] Though these may mean that the scheme would work somewhat differently, they cannot be counted as objections weighty enough to warrant pronouncing judgment against its introduction. Federal systems, such as those in India, Canada and Australia, of course need ombudsmen at both levels of government, and the size and population of some countries might call for a collegial body, an Ombudsman Commission, as I have dubbed it. Otherwise, as New Zealand's experience has demonstrated, an ombudsman can be fitted into the Commonwealth parliamentary system with only minor adjustments, and even some of these, designed to assuage the sensitivity of ministers, were not necessary. We should hold out strongly against irrelevant arguments about the ombudsman's supposed interference with ministerial responsibility, for they are likely to result in an undesirable limitation upon his power to investigate and criticize.

More relevant than Professor Abel's objections, it seems to me, is Professor Mitchell's complaint in the same volume that an ombudsman would not be enough. Certainly the scheme can not claim to solve completely the difficult problems of preventing executive arbitrariness and securing redress in the modern democratic state. Administrative procedures themselves must be improved, parliamentary control must be strengthened, free legal aid must be made more widely available, review by the courts must be simplified and perhaps extended, and much wider opportunities must be provided for appealing administrative decisions. In common law countries one is tempted to take the view, as does Professor Mitchell, that drastic reform in the direction of the European administrative courts is required. But one need not therefore conclude that the ombudsman scheme is undesirable, claiming it is only a poor substitute for administrative courts. As I have already suggested, the two may be regarded as half-loaves that together make up the whole.

Unfortunately, many of the reforms that are needed are in the complex realm of administrative and legal procedure and are not easily understood by the public. Hence pressure upon governments for reforms tends to be weak. Yet governments are not prone to proposing on their own volition measures that limit their own executive powers. One of the great virtues of the ombudsman idea is that its simplicity gives it tremendous popular appeal. The public enthusiasm engendered by discussing it is likely to overflow into support for other desirable reforms in more legally technical areas.

When one looks comparatively at democratic systems in the modern world one finds a surprising degree of uniformity in their basic governmental machinery and institutions - the representative assembly, the responsible and/or elected executive, the independent courts, the legislative financial auditor, the secret ballot, the public corporation, etc. Machinery that has proved its worth in one country has been gradually adopted in the others. Yet in the modern history of democratic government the invention of new institutional devices has been rare. The secret ballot and the public corporation are among the few that might be said to fall into this category. It is true that technically the ombudsman system cannot be described as a new invention, for it was created in 1809. But its transformation in recent times into an institution whose primary function is to supervise the administration, has given it a new dimension and character.

Hence, the ombudsman should be regarded as an important new addition to the armoury of democratic government. Like the legislative auditor, he enhances the control and prestige of legislature in a world in which executive power is growing. Indeed, after New Zealand had paved the way by demonstrating that this Scandinavian scheme could be successfully exported to other countries, I was willing to predict that the ombudsman institution or its equivalent would become a standard part of the machinery of government through the democratic world.

Footnotes - Chapter 7

1.   Albert Abel, "Commonwealth Constitutional
Complications," in Donald C. Rowat, ed., <u>The Ombudsman</u>
(London: Allen & Unwin; Toronto: University of Toronto
Press, 2nd ed., 1968), 281-87.

8.

Having seen that the ombudsman plan can adapt successfully
to differing constitutional and legal systems, let us now
turn to some controversial questions that must be answered
in the course of transplanting it: Should the ombudsman be
able to criticize not only the fairness but also the reasonableness of decisions? Should he be able to criticize the
actions of cabinet ministers? Should a minister be empowered
to stop an investigation, and should complaints come to the
ombudsman only through members of parliament, as the Whyatt
Report proposed? How should the ombudsman be appointed?
Should he have the power to prosecute officials? And, finally, should he supervise the courts or local governments?
On several of these questions, as we have seen, the Nordic
countries themselves differ.

The question of the power to criticize the reasonableness of discretionary decisions is perhaps the most controversial. Denmark and Norway have given the ombudsman this
power maybe because, like the English-speaking countries,
they have no system of administrative courts. If the ombudsman is given this power, one problem is that he may take up
cases for which there are already adequate facilities for
administrative appeal, thus extending his work unnecessarily
and creating confusion. For this reason the New Zealand law
states that he shall have no jurisdiction over any decision
on which there is already a right of appeal on its merits,
and the Danish law was changed in 1959 to provide that he
shall not have jurisdiction over any such decision except
for faulty administrative procedure or conduct. Either of
these provisions would solve the problem, although the second is preferable because of the unregulated nature of the
administrative procedure.

Another problem, however, is that in many discretionary
situations any one of several decisions may be reasonable,
or the decision may involve a question of policy. Hence
there is the danger that an ombudsman may merely substitute
his views on the merits of a decision for that of an experienced official or regulatory body, or even of the responsible minister, thus perhaps wandering into a politically
controversial field and endandering the prestige of the

institution. And yet, because of the common lack of facilities for appealing discretionary decisions, and because courts and tribunals are unsuitable for appeals on many types of discretionary decision, the need for more adequate control is great. My own view is that the ombudsman should be given this power to criticize reasonableness, but in such a way that he can use it only in cases of patent unreasonableness, as the ombudsman in Denmark has done. It should not be beyond the wit of legal draftsmen to devise a wording that would suit. Perhaps the wording in the legislation for Norway and New Zealand could be used as a guide. In New Zealand, however, the provision that he may criticize not only a decision that he thinks is "unreasonable" but simply "wrong" seems to be too broad.[1]

On the second question, the ombudsman may criticize the actions of individual ministers in Norway, Finland, and Denmark, and indeed has done so in a number of cases. In Sweden, however, although he may prosecute a minister at the direction of parliament, otherwise he has no formal authority to investigate the actions of ministers because of the divorce between the administration and the ministry, and because constitutionally the latter acts collectively and its decisions are those of the King. In New Zealand and Britain, too, the parliamentary commissioner has no power to investigate ministers, no doubt because of the fear that this might interfere with their responsibility to parliament. However, just how the power to criticize the legality of a minister's decisions might interfere with ministerial responsibility has never been clearly explained. Certainly, an auditor general's power to criticize has not done so. Obviously, ministers are fallible human beings capable of making unjust decisions, using arbitrary procedures and taking illegal action. Under a system of cabinet dominance and secrecy, they may easily do so without parliament's knowledge. We must keep in mind, too, that the minister usually sides with his officials on administrative decisions. The ombudsman should not be authorized, of course, to comment on decisions of the whole cabinet, or on matters of policy, or politics, and he should have no power to interfere with a minister's decisions, but only to get at the facts of those decisions and report on them critically to parliament. This would be an aid to parliament's control over the executive rather than the reverse. Hence, I favour giving this power to the ombudsman, in the belief that it will be used wisely and impartially, as in the Nordic countries.

For the same reasons one cannot agree with the proposals of the Whyatt Report that a minister should be empowered to stop an investigation or refuse to release departmental minutes to the parliamentary commissioner. After all, he is an officer of parliament, and surely can be trusted with confidential information. To function effectively, he must have power to get at all the facts of a case. There is a vast difference between making information available to the ombudsman and making it available to the public. He should of course not be empowered to disclose state secrets or information injurious to private persons or firms. The Whyatt Report justified its restrictive proposals with the argument that the freedom to investigate might interfere with Britain's long-established system of ministerial responsibility, whereas a comparable ministerial system was not introduced in Denmark until 1953 and presumably still was not firmly established. But Miss Pedersen, a Danish judge, has pointed out in reply that this simply is not true. The system of ministerial responsibility was introduced in Denmark as long ago as 1849, and the ombudsman system has worked smoothly there without these proposed restrictions.[2]

Nor can one agree with the Whyatt proposal that members of parliament should become a kind of buffer between the citizens and the parliamentary commissioner. One of the great advantages of the ombudsman scheme is its direct and easy access. There can be no objection to citizens complaining in the first instance to their members, but there is no good reason why this should be required. In some cases the aggrieved citizen will know and wish to deal with his member but in many others he will not, especially because of the member's political partisanship. There should be as many avenues as possible for receiving complaints. The parliamentary commissioner could instead be required to pass to the relevant member copies of all complaints received, indicating in each case whether he intends to investigate. This would satisfy the desirable principle that under a system of single-member constituencies, the relevant member should be kept informed and should provide what help he can. If reducing the number of frivolous complaints was the main consideration behind the Whyatt proposal, the initial requirement in New Zealand's law that the complaint must be accompanied by a small fee (£1) would have met the problem. Even if it is agreed that for an initial period the members should screen all complaints in order to reduce their number, the assumption that the members would then continue to be a buffer is unacceptable. It is stated in the Report (p. 72) that the commissioner need not inform the complainant of his decision, and may leave this to the member. But as Miss Pedersen has pointed out, once an investigation has begun, the complainant ought to be a direct party to the proceedings in his own right.[3]

On the question of appointment of the ombudsman it is clear that he should be appointed by the legislature, as in New Zealand, in order to enhance his independent position, even though under a strong tradition of executive appointment he would probably be proposed by the executive. That he should be chosen by a multi-party committee of parliament, as in Sweden, is perhaps too much to expect. In the Nordic countries the ombudsman's appointment is for only a short term, usually the life of a parliament. Though often he is reappointed, sometimes he is not. Short-term appointment is not such a danger to the ombudsman's independence under a multi-party system as it would be under a system of strong majority governments. The New Zealand bill copied the Danish scheme too slavishly in this respect. Under a strong majority system a government would be tempted to replace the ombudsman when it came to power, and if this should happen, it could easily ruin the scheme. For this reason, he should be appointed with long tenure, and probably should have the same security as judges. To further ensure his independence, he should report to a special parliamentary committee, as the auditor general does to a committee on public accounts in the Commonwealth countries, and the chairman of the committee should be a member of the opposition. As with the office of auditor general, the success of the scheme will depend greatly on the nature of this committee and on how vigorously it deals with the ombudsman's reports.

The questions of whether the ombudsman should have power to prosecute, as in Finland and Sweden, or to order a prosecution as in Denmark, are more difficult to answer. These powers have been omitted from the Norwegian, New Zealand and most subsequent plans. It is clear that the ombudsmen's power to prosecute is much more important as a threat than an action. In Finland and Sweden they actually prosecute only about seven or eight cases a year, but may virtually force their views upon officials through the threat of prosecution. This can have the undesirable effect that in serious cases remedial action may be secured in a rather informal manner without recourse to and pronouncement by the courts. In any case the power to prosecute does not seem crucial, for without it an ombudsman is still able publicly to recommend a prosecution.

Whether the ombudsman should have the power to supervise the courts is a more controversial question. This power, too, was omitted from the Danish and later plans. Yet it is significant that at least a quarter of the Swedish ombudsman's cases deal with complaints about the courts and public prosecutors. The courts were excluded in Denmark partly because there had already been created within the court system a special court to deal with complaints. Regarding the argument for judicial independence, an eminent Swedish ombudsman had this to say:

> I myself come from the ranks of judges, and can assure that I have never heard a Swedish judge complain that his independent and unattached position is endangered by the fact that the JO [ombudsman] may examine his activity in office. To claim an independent position does not necessarily mean that a judge should be free from responsibility or criticism when acting against the law. From the JO's annual reports of the past 150 years, anybody may see that there has been a need for the supervision of judges also. [4]

It is important to note that the Swedish ombudsman who deals with the courts does not set himself up as a general appeal body reviewing the substance of cases, but instead deals specifically with maladministration within the court system, with complaints about such matters as delay or the faulty behaviour of judges. Yet he handles more than three hundred such complaints a year. Clearly it is not healthy to pretend that our judges can do no wrong. It seems reasonable to propose either that the ombudsman should be given jurisdiction over the courts, or that there should be created within the court system a special office or court for complaints, as in Denmark. If the first proposal raises fears for the independence of the courts, the ombudsman could be required to send his serious criticisms of judicial action to a disciplinary authority within the court system, such as the chief justice, rather than to parliament; minor criticisms would of course go direct to the judge concerned.

Finally, there is the question of whether the ombudsman's competence should extend to municipal councils and officers. The ombudsman supervises municipalities in Finland, Sweden extended the ombudsman's jurisdiction to local governments in 1957, and Denmark did likewise in 1961, followed by Norway and New Zealand in 1969 and 1976. The Whyatt Committee found numerous examples of uncontrolled discretionary powers at the local level in Britain, and proposed the eventual inclusion of local government in the British scheme. After establishing a national plan in 1967, Great Britain set up a separate scheme for local governments in 1974-75, with two complaints commissioners for local administration in England, one in Scotland, and one in Wales. It seems reasonable to conclude that either a national ombudsman plan should include local governments or a separate scheme should be set up for them, though perhaps elected members of councils and boards should be exempted from their supervision, along with cities or counties that are large enough to have an ombudman of their own.

Footnotes - Chapter Eight

1. The 1961 bill is reprinted in the Whyatt Report, Appendix B. Under Sec. 18 the commissioner make take action with respect to any decision, recommendation, act or omission where he finds that it: (a) appears to have been contrary to law; or (b) was unreasonable, unjust, oppressive, or improperly discriminatory, or was in accordance with a rule of law or a provision of any enactment or a practice that it is or may be unreasonable, unjust, oppressive, or improperly discriminatory; or (c) was based wholly or partly on a mistake of law or fact; or (d) was wrong; or (e) involved the exercise of discretionary power for an improper purpose or on irrelevant grounds or on the taking into account of irrelevant considerations or where reasons should have been given for the decision. These provisions remained unchanged in the 1962 act.

2. I.M. Pedersen, "The Parliamentary Commissioner: A Danish View," Public Law, CXXIV, 1 (Spring, 1962), 18.

3. Ibid.

4. Alfred Bexelius, "The Swedish Institution of the Justitieombudsman," International Review of Administrative Sciences XXVII, 3 (1961), 245. For another strong argument in favour of the ombudsman's supervision over the courts, see C.-A. Sheppard, "An Ombudsman for Canada," McGill Law Journal 10, 4 (1964), 291-340.

PART THREE:
OMBUDSMEN IN
NORTH AMERICA

9.

THE CASE FOR THE PLAN
IN THE USA

This brief chapter is intended to show why the ombudsman institution is needed in the United States. My main contention is that the United States is at much the same stage in the evolution of the administrative state as the advanced countries that first adopted the institution. Therefore the conditions calling for its adoption are much the same.

What are these conditions and why is the ombudsman system considered necessary to meet them? In this century there has been a tremendous growth in the range and complexity of government activities, particularly since the war. This growth has brought an increasing likelihood of bureaucratic red tape, delay and mistakes. It has also brought increasing powers of discretion to officials and thus an increasing opportunity for them to be arbitrary and unfair.

The trouble is that we have been lulled by the progress of modern science into the thought that similar progress is proceeding in realms of law and administration, and that therefore nothing can go wrong. We are like the man who was greatly impressed with modern automation, and who went to take the first flight of a completely automatic jet-powered aircraft from New York to Tokyo. As he walked into the aircraft, he felt a little eerie because he could see no stewardesses, and there was not even a door to the pilot's cabin. But he sat down and wondered what was going to happen next. Then there came over the public address system the following recorded message: "This is the first automated jet flight from New York to Tokyo. We are about to take off, so please fasten your seatbelts and extinguish your cigarettes. There is no pilot on this aircraft, but just sit back and relax, and don't worry, because nothing can go wrong - go wrong - go wrong - go wrong - go wrong - go wrong..."! We may be similarly under the comfortable illusion that, because governments today are supposedly using modern scientific techniques of administration, nothing can go wrong.

The United States has a strong tradition of protecting individual rights, but other developed democratic countries are beginning to overtake it in providing protections against administrative injustice. While Scandinavia has developed the ombudsman scheme, other West European countries have extended their systems of administrative courts to deal with abuses of executive power. The United Kingdom not only has been taking active measures to control and improve administrative adjudication, but has preceded the United States in adopting a version of the ombudsman plan at the national level.

It is also my contention that the differences between the United States and the countries that first adopted the ombudsman system are not great enough to override the common conditions that call for its adoption. These differences would, of course, require certain obvious adjustments to the scheme. Thus, because of the federal system of government in the United States, there would need to be an ombudsman for each of the states as well as for the federal government.

American opponents of the plan have worried about overlap and conflict of jurisdiction between federal and state ombudsmen. But these are not serious problems because ombudsmen do not have executive power. Since they have only advisory powers, if a federal ombudsman received a complaint having to do with a decision made by a state authority, and proceeded to deal with it anyway, no harm would be done. He would make only a recommendation. If the case were to be challenged in a court as infringing on state powers under the constitution, the court would not have a very good ground to limit his action, because the action would not be executive or juducial. He would have made no binding decision of any kind, and a state authority would be free to ignore his recommendation.

With ombudsmen at both levels of government, it is true that complaints will often be sent to the wrong ombudsman. Under a federal system, confused citizens often don't know which level of government is responsible for what. Legislators and officials often mistakenly receive complaints about decisions at other levels of government. Hence, the ombudsmen at both levels are likely to receive a number of complaints that should have gone to the other level. A situation like this exists in Australia, where there are both federal and state ombudsmen. Complaints are often sent to the ombudsman at the wrong level of government. In some cases the same complaint will even be sent to both levels. But the ombudsmen keep in touch with one another and trade information; they see that the complaint is transferred to the proper office, and inform the citizen that this has been done. Having ombudsmen at both levels of government doesn't create any problem of duplication. Indeed, it actually helps uneducated and bewildered citizens to find out which level of government they should deal with.

It has been argued that because of the large population of the United States, the institution would turn into a vast bureaucracy in its own right. However, the existence of multiple ombudsmen in a federal system would automatically prevent this. Anyway, ombudsman offices require a very small professional staff. It is unlikely that a federal ombudsman office in the United States would require a professional staff of much more than a hundred. This staff could specialize in different types of cases and would provide far more effective service than the present costly and often untrained staffs of individual congressmen. Regional offices would probably be required, though travel from Washington might be an adequate substitute since national ombudsmen have little difficulty in conducting their operations almost entirely by mail and inspection tours.

For large countries like the United States I have suggested a collegial ombudsman body, the members of which could travel separately and specialize in various types of administration. They could personally investigate a much larger volume of complaints than a single ombudsman. On important and complex cases they would probably render a fairer judgment and the weight of their combined authority would be greater. However, there might be a greater danger of partisanship in their appointment, since each party would want to name members. In the case of a single ombudsman, the majority party might be willing to agree to a joint, nonpartisan appointment. If it were not willing, the appointment to a plural body of an equal number of members by each party would be a lesser evil than a single, partisan ombudsman because they would cancel each other's partisanship.

It may be thought that the great differences between the parliamentary or cabinet system of government and the constitutional separation of powers in the United States would create circumstances that make the ombudsman institution difficult to transplant to that country. However, the only constitutional limits the American system would place upon an ombudsman as an agent of Congress are that he could not be granted the power to prosecute in the courts, and his power to investigate may be somewhat limited by the doctrine of "executive privilege." The power to prosecute is not essential to the scheme in any case; his freedom to recommend a prosecution would be almost as affective. And, clearly, an ombudsman's office would have more ability and power to get at the facts of a case than any individual congressman has at present. Because of the tradition of judicial supremacy in the United States, the office might become involved in some minor litigation over its powers and procedures, but a court could not seriously restrict its powers since they are only advisory.

The greatest dangers to the success of the scheme in the United States are that it may be discredited by being adopted as an executive office, which would be too much under the control of the chief executive, or in a form that may subject it to too much partisan pressure. At the state or city level, it could even be captured by a political machine. The institution will work well only in a reasonably well-administered state or city; where a civil service is riddled with patronage or corruption, it couldn't cope with the situation single-handed.

In the American system of dispersed power, multiple pressure points, pressure group politics and legislative-executive tension, all agencies of government tend to be tinged with partisanship or bias, or at least are suspected of being so. Care would therefore have to be taken to make the ombudsman absolutely independent, so that he could not be accused of becoming a fixer for some private interest, or of conducting a fishing expedition for congressmen, or of white-washing the administration. The Reuss bill,[1] for example, provided that cases should come to the ombudsman (called the Legislative Counsel) only by reference from members of Congress. But access to the ombudsman should not be controlled by the caprices of individual congressmen, nor should their direct pressures upon the ombudsman be encouraged in this way. The institution could be set up as a body appointed jointly by Congress and the President, but this would radically change the nature of the scheme and would run the danger not only of partisan appointment but also of too much control by the executive.

The concept of the ombudsman institution as an agency of the legislature fits in well with the American separation of powers because one of the main jobs of the legislature is to act as a check on the adminisration. A legislative ombudsman under the separation of powers would not run the same danger as under the cabinet system of being dominated by the executive. Unlike the cabinet system, in which the ministers are collectively responsible for the whole administration and sit in the legislature where they can be directly controlled and questioned about administrative matters, the system of separated powers provides no easy way for the legislature to check on the administration. Considering the looseness of the chief executive's control over the administrative agencies, and their steadily growing number and size at both levels of government, such a check is badly needed. Federal and state ombudsmen would help to meet that need.

Footnotes - Chapter Nine

1. Filed by Congressman Reuss in several successive sessions of the House of Representatives. The bill as introduced in 1963 (H.R. 7593) is reprinted in the appendix to <u>The Ombudsman</u>, <u>op. cit.</u>

10

RECENT DEVELOPMENTS
IN THE USA

After 1965 a remarkable burgeoning of interest in ombudsman-
ship occurred in the United States. Indeed, one might almost
call it 'ombudsmania.' As one commentator put it in 1966,
"The Word this year is Ombudsman!" On December 2, 1966, Time
magazine ran a story headed "The People's Watchdog," featur-
ing the two new books on the subject by Walter Gellhorn,
eminent Professor of Law at Columbia University. Accompanying the story was a photograph of the "Om-" column from Webster's unabridged dictionary, to which were added a red in-
sert mark and the word 'Om-budsman,' written into the appropriate place in the column. Time claimed that "so far, the
word does not even appear in U.S. dictionaries." To its dis-
may, it received letters from Funk and Wagnalls and Thorn-
dyke-Barnhart pointing out that the word appeared in their
dictionaries! Quoth red-faced Time in its next issue: "Time
is wordless. Ombudsman can also be found in the addendum of
Webster's third, unabridged." Also significant is the fact
that in Congressman Reuss's ombudsman bill, reintroduced as
HR 3388 on January 23, 1967, the name of the proposed Administrative Counsel was changed to Congressional Ombudsman.

In 1965, in the Introduction to The Ombudsman, I predic-
ted that, even though Canada and the United States had taken
an interest in the ombudsman plan more recently than had
Britain, they were likely to create a version of it more
quickly because it could be adopted at either the national
or the provincial or state level of government. In the
event, this turned out to be true, but only partly true,
because I had not anticipated that the first adoption might
be at the local level. The first jurisdiction to create a
version of the office was Nassau County, N.Y. On May 31,
1966, the county executive, a Democrat, appointed to the
office of commissioner of accounts a person to act as Public
Protector, and gave him authority to "protect the public and
individual citizens against inefficiency, maladministration,
arrogance, abuse, and other failures of government." The
person appointed was formerly a judge and chairman of the
county board of ethics. By the end of May 1967, he had handled about 500 cases. Meanwhile, however, the county's board
of supervisors, which was predominantly Republican, had
appointed an advisory committee on the ombudsman, with the
county prosecutor as chairman. After a trip to Scandinavia,

he recommended that the Public Protector should become an agent of the legislative rather than the executive branch of the county's government; he should be appointed by the board of supervisors and, to ensure his political neutrality and independence, should be removable only by a two-thirds vote of the board. [1] But these proposals were not adopted. Although the Public Protector was popularly referred to as an ombudsman, he did not meet the essential qualification of being an independent agency of the legislative branch.

The State-Level Ombudsmen

More significant was the adoption of genuine ombudsman plans at the state level by Hawaii, Nebraska, Iowa and Alaska. Hawaii's ombudsman bill was approved by the legislature on April 30, 1967, and sent to the state governor for signature. Under the provisions of Hawaii's constitution, since the bill was approved within the last ten days of the session, it automatically became law on June 24th, even though Governor Burns refused to sign it. Since the ombudsman was to be elected by the legislature, the scheme did not come into operation until the 1968 session. Herman S. Doi, former head of Hawaii's legislative reference bureau, was chosen for the post. Late in 1965, the reference bureau had produced a brief report on ombudsmen, which reprinted the acts for Denmark and New Zealand, the bill for Connecticut (the first bill drafted for a state), and a model state bill produced by the Harvard Student Legislative Research Bureau. These clearly formed the basis for drafting Hawaii's legislation. Though all of them are similar, a comparison reveals that Hawaii's act is based mainly on the Harvard bill, except that the former wisely provides for the ombudsman to be elected by the legislature rather than appointed by the governor. He is elected for a six-year term and has been re-elected twice. A two-thirds vote in both houses is needed to remove him from office. To make the office accessible throughout Hawaii, he makes periodic visits to the outer islands. He also pioneered the practice of encouraging complaints to be made by collect long-distance telephone calls. As a result, a very large proportion of his complaints are initiated by telephone. This practice was later followed by other state ombudsmen.

In 1969 and 1972 Nebraska and Iowa approved similar acts for a legislative ombudsman, formally named the Public Counsel in Nebraska and the Citizens' Aide in Iowa, but popularly called ombudsmen. Thus Nebraska and Iowa became the first mainland American states to have a genuine ombudsman. In Nebraska he is appointed for six years and in Iowa for four, and can be removed only by a two-thirds vote of the legisla-

ture.   Nebraska's first ombudsman, Murrell McNeil, was formerly state tax commissioner, while the first one in Iowa,
Lawrence Carstensen, had been a county attorney and an as-
semblyman.

In 1975 Alaska became the fourth state to adopt the
plan, and Francis M. Flavin, a lawyer, was elected as ombudsman for a six-year term.   An interesting feature of
Alaska's plan is that a municipality may join it by passing
an ordinance, though the city of Anchorage has its own plan,
dating from 1974.

In addition to these four states, the Commonwealth of
Puerto Rico and the Territory of Guam set up legislative
offices in 1977 and 1979.   As a way of reaching the public,
Puerto Rico's ombudsman began a program of visits throughout
the island in 1979.

For the six state-level plans, the number of complaints
and enquiries received per year ranges from about 1,000 in
Guam and Nebraska to nearly 8,000 in Puerto Rico.

Federal-Level Developments

At the federal level, Senator Long introduced a bill in
March 1967 (S. 1195) to create an Administrative Ombudsman
who, unlike the Congressional Ombudsman in the Reuss proposal, would receive complaints directly rather than through
Congressmen, but whose jurisdiction would be restricted
initially to a few agencies such as the Social Security and
Veterans Administrations.   Earlier, Senator Long and two co-
sponsors had introduced a bill for an ombudsman in the District of Columbia.   Senators Magnuson and Long also filed a
Tax Ombudsman Bill, but this was really a proposal to create
regional commissioners within the Tax Court to decide appeals on small tax claims.

In February 1967 Congressman Reuss decided to dramatize
his ombudsman bill and test the ombudsman idea by appointing
a personal assistant as a temporary 'ombudsman' for his
Milwaukee constituency.   Professors Gellhorn and Anderson
and I agreed to act as consultants on the project.   The
assistant held office hours at six postal stations as well
as in a central office. Over a four-month period he received
nearly 500 complaints and enquiries requiring some form of
action.   Most of these were by telephone or personal call,
with very few by mail.   Surprisingly, 40 per cent of them
concerned state or local government.   A large number of the
complaints were justified, many of them cases of administrative delay. Backed by Mr. Reuss's influence, the 'ombudsman'

85

had good success with remedial action. At the end of the project the assistant prepared a brief analysis of the results, in which he not unexpectedly recommended the Reuss proposal for the screening of complaints by Congressmen.

In October 1967 the American Assembly chose the ombudsman as the subject of its national conference, and the background papers later became the book edited by Stanley Anderson, Ombudsmen for American Government? The conference also issued a brief report favouring ombudsmen for state and local governments and experimentation with the idea at the federal level. The subject was also discussed at regional conferences of the Assembly throughout the following year. The American Bar Association also took up the idea, and its section on Administrative Law formed an Ombudsmen Committee under the enthusiastic and able chairmanship of Bernard Frank. At the initiative of this Committee, the Bar Association in 1969 adopted a resolution similarly favouring ombudsmen for state and local governments and experimentation at the federal level. It proposed that the Administrative Conference of the United States, a body created to review and recommend improvements in administrative procedures, should experiment by constituting itself an ombudsman for limited areas of federal activity and should encourage and study experimentation with the idea. The Administrative Conference, however, was not adequately equipped to take on more than a very limited complaint-handling role, though it was willing to encourage studies of and experiments with the ombudsman idea. In 1971, for instance, it launched a study of how complaints are handled by federal agencies and departments. The Bar Association resolution was amended in July 1971 to make clear that experimentation at the federal level should not be restricted to the Administrative Conference.

During the 1970's, various additional legislative proposals were made at the federal level. Unfortunately some of these departed from the original ombudsman concept. In March 1972, for instance, Congressman Aspin introduced a bill to provide each member of the House of Representatives with an "ombudsman," who would be trained and assisted by a proposed Ombudsman Center in Washington. These so-called ombudsmen, to be paid only up to $15,000 per year, would be little more than errand boys for House members.

Regarding proposals that are closer to the original concept, the approach has been to propose an experimental plan of limited scope because of a fear that a full-blown ombudsman institution would itself turn into a cumbersome bureaucracy, and would lack the expertise necessary to deal with the myriad of specialized agencies at the federal level. Thus in 1971 Senator Javits, along with four other Senators, and Representatives Steiger and Reuss, introduced in the Senate and House similar bills called the Administrative Ombudsman Experimentation Act (S. 2200 and H.R. 9562). This Act would add to the Economic Opportunity Act of 1964 a section providing for an ombudsman who would be limited to demonstration projects in three regions and to programs directed at the low-income groups, in fields such as education, health and employment. At the same time, there would be an American Ombudsman Foundation, which would initiate and support ombudsman research and demonstration projects among state and local governments. The ombudsman would be appointed by the Speaker of the House and the President of the Senate after consultation with the majority and minority leaders, while the Foundation's fifteen-man board would be appointed by the President with the advice and consent of the Senate. Also, in April 1972, Representative Ryan introduced a bill (H.R. 14338) to restrict grants under the Omnibus Crime Control and Safe Streets Act of 1968 to states that appoint "correctional ombudsmen" for prisoners, parolees and probationers.

During this period, too, the federal Office of Economic Opportunity funded ombudsman studies and complaint-handling experiments by state and local governments, notably in cooperation with the University of California, whose Institute of Governmental Studies at Berkeley and Ombudsman Activities Project at Santa Barbara have pioneered research and activities on the subject in the United States. Thus the OEO initially supported the Nebraska plan, and the schemes for Iowa, Dayton, Buffalo, Newark and Seattle, discussed below. It also supported what may turn out to have been an historic occasion: the first conference of the American ombudsmen. This was a workshop organized by the director of the Ombudsman Activities Project, Stanley Anderson, and held at Seattle in August 1972. It was attended by OEO and Project officers, academic ombudsman-watchers like myself, two foreign ombudsmen, and five genuine American state and local ombudsmen.

Other State-Level Developments

Because of the magnitude of the problems encountered at the federal level, a full-scale federal plan is not likely to be adopted, at least for some years. More likely will be further adoptions at the state and local levels. By 1968 legislators had filed ombudsman bills in over half of the states, while by 1971 they had filed about 50 ombudsman bills of various kinds in 33 of the states, including such important states as California, Illinois and New York. Around 1975, however, there began a rapid decline in the popularity of general legislative ombudsmen for states. After Alaska's adoption in 1975, no new general legislative plans had been adopted by 1982. This may be partly explained by a shift in favour of ombudsmen appointed by the state governors, and by the growing popularity of ombudsmen for particular services such as institutional care, where the need was clearest.

At the end of 1966 the newly elected Lieutenant Governor of Colorado, a Democrat in a predominantly Republican state, announced that, like an ombudsman, he was prepared to receive and investigate complaints. By the end of May 1967, he had received about 500 complaints and enquiries. The Lieutenant Governor of Illinois similarly decided to handle complaints on his own initiative, while in New Mexico the Lieutenant Governor was given specific powers to receive and refer complaints, through legislation passed in 1971. The Governor of Oregon appointed an ombudsman in 1969 by executive order. Similar offices were created in Iowa (1970) and South Carolina (1971). Iowa's office was funded by the OEO, was set up in cooperation with the University of California's Ombudsman Activities Project, and was succeeded in 1972 by the earlier-mentioned legislative office, but with the same incumbent.

Although one or two of these executive complaint schemes were set up partly to give a push to the idea of a legislative ombudsman, unfortunately they made one appear to be unnecessary, and were influential as precedents for other states. Thus many of the state bills mentioned above proposed an ombudsman appointed and virtually controlled by the chief executive.

During the 1970's many governors set up central information and referral services, some of which also handle complaints, often with a toll-free telephone service. Counting these complaint services, by 1982 there were executive central complaint offices in about twelve of the states. These and the new central information and referral services seem to be regarded as an alternative to legislative ombudsmen, even though they do not have the same functions.

Similarly, after 1975 the idea of ombudsmen for special purposes partly eclipsed that of a general ombudsman. Thus by 1982 special ombudsman plans for correctional institutions had been established in 18 states. And under a federal law of 1978 all states had set up ombudsman programs for long-term care institutions. Much effort went into the design of these programs, to the neglect of the idea of a general ombudsman.

Local Developments

At the local level, the developments in New York city during 1966 and 1967 were of great significance in promoting the ombudsman idea. In November 1966 the Civilian Review Board for investigating complaints against the city police was abolished in a bitterly fought referendum. The Policemen's Benevolent Association, which took the stand that such a board should not single out the police, is reported to have spent $400,000 in the campaign against Mayor Lindsay's support of the Board. After the Board's defeat, both sides agreed that a version of the ombudsman institution, which would be able to review complaints against any part of the civic administration, might be a suitable compromise. The ombudsman idea was already well known there because Judge Bexelius, Sweden's ombudsman, and Sir Guy Powles, New Zealand's ombudsman, had crossed paths in New York during tours of the United States early in 1966. In the course of his tour Judge Bexelius had also given evidence before committees of the Congress and the California legislature. In New York, the two ombudsmen appeared simultaneously at a meeting chaired by Professor Gellhorn in a kind of all-star show before the powerful local bar association. Bills on the subject had also been submitted to the City Council.

Mayor Lindsay therefore referred the idea to a team of city officials to draft a plan. Later, however, he re-introduced his scheme for city-wide Neighborhood City Halls, which would be run by the executive branch on a budget of $250,000. The Democratically controlled city council opposed this scheme for fear it would be used for political purposes. In May 1967 the local bar association produced a draft bill for an independent ombudsman, to be appointed with the advice and consent of two-thirds of the Council and removed only for cause by a three-quarters vote. The President of the Council immediately supported and introduced the bill, but Mayor Lindsay's reaction was to favour instead expanding the office of the Commissioner of Investigation, who was an executive officer, and making his appointment subject to Council approval. Partly as a result, the bill was not approved.

However, New York's new city charter, which became effective in January 1977, provided for a version of the legislative ombudsman plan. The president of the city council is to be the ombudsman. Paul L. Dwyer, a strong advocate of the ombudsman plan, was the first to hold the office. The ombudsman's functions are to coordinate city-wide complaint programs, review recurring complaints, and propose better complaint procedures.

Other developments have also given a strong push toward ombudsman adoptions for cities. In July 1966 the law school at the University of Buffalo began a pilot project under two professors as unofficial ombudsmen for the city of Buffalo. This project, which ran for eighteen months, was highly successful, carefully analyzed and widely reported. Early in 1967 Professor Gellhorn produced a model ombudsman bill for state and local governments, and in March 1967 the President's Commission on Law Enforcement and Administration of Justice recommended replacing local police review boards with general "ombudsman-type" complaint agencies.

As a result of this popularization of the ombudsman idea, numerous ombudsman proposals and adoptions have been made in many cities, and various related complaint-handling mechanisms have been developed. In some cities, such as Philadelphia and Flint, private organizations took up the Buffalo precedent by establishing an unofficial "community ombudsman." Because of the long history of complaint bureaus in American city administration, a common official reaction to the ombudsman idea has been for the mayor or city manager to appoint a complaint officer as part of his office and call him an ombudsman. Such an officer can only be a pale shadow of a real legislative ombudsman.

The Ombudsmen for Local Government

Progress has been made with genuine ombudsmen for local government, however. It should be noted that municipalities can come under the state plan in Alaska, and that the ombudsmen in Hawaii and Iowa have jurisdiction over local government, including mayors and councillors. Some of the state bills would also give the state ombudsman supervision over local government, while others propose separate ombudsmen at the county level. A similar proposal has been made for the province of Ontario in Canada, to create provincially appointed ombudsmen for local government at a regional level.

Two of the first ombudsman plans to be adopted at the local level were joint city-county schemes: Dayton-Montgomery County in Ohio, and Seattle-King County in Washington. The Dayton-Montgomery scheme, set up in March 1971 with financial support from the OEO and the Kettering Foundation, has a joint office of citizen complaints headed by a director and a supervisory ombudsman board. The members of the board are appointed by Dayton's city council, Dayton's school board and Montgomery County's board of commissioners. The ombudsman board elects the director and approves the budget. It may dismiss the director, but only by a two-thirds vote. The director handles complaints against the administration of the city, the school board or the county. The first director, T. Bingham, a former newsman, publicized his office by presenting interesting cases on TV and in the press. Hence the volume of complaints, mostly by telephone, was large from the start. In recent years, there have been about 3,000 complaints plus nearly 6,000 enquiries per year.

The Seattle-King County plan originated with an office of citizen complaints for King County only, which began in January 1970. Arrangements were then made for a joint city-county scheme, set up under an ordinance approved by the councils of both governments in July 1970. This ordinance, which is based on Professor Gellhorn's model ombudsman bill, provides for a joint office of citizen complaints, with a director appointed for five years by a two-thirds majority vote of each council and removable only by a similar two thirds vote. He must be selected from a list of at least five names submitted by a citizens' advisory commission, and in formulating policies and procedures he is assisted by an advisory committee of three members from each council. The first director, L. Walton, was a former city manager. When the second director left office in 1979, he was replaced by two ombudsmen, one appointed by the city council and one by the county council. In 1982 Seattle withdrew from the joint scheme.

With the help of federal funding, Newark, N.J., in May 1972 became one of the first American cities to provide for a legislative ombudsman. To be appointed for five years by the mayor, with the consent of the city council, he could be removed only by a two-thirds vote of the council. The plan was approved by a council vote of only six to three, and the federal funding covered only two years, so it was not established on very firm foundations. In October the council rejected Mayor Gibson's choice for ombudsman by a vote of six to two, some councillors using arguments which revealed that they were opposed to the plan rather than the man, who was a professor of law and had been reared in Newark. Interpreting this to mean that the council did not wish to implement the plan, Mayor Gibson announced in October that he was returning the federal grant of $262,000.

This early failure illustrates that the establishment of local plans is often subjected to the vagaries of partisan politics. Combined with the tendency of executive heads to set up their own complaint offices, the result has been slow progress in establishing legislative plans. However, several more have been adopted, mainly during the period 1970-75. By July 1982, there were twelve local schemes classed by the International Ombudsman Institute as independent legislative ones. Besides the two city-county schemes already described, one of these was for a county: Cuyahoga, Ohio (1980). The largest cities with a legislative plan were, besides New York: Detroit, Mich. (1973); Flint, Mich. (1974); Atlanta, Ga. (1974); and Berkeley, Cal. (1975).

The ombudsman idea has become so widespread in the United States that ombudsmen have been appointed for universities, school systems, hospitals and other public and private organizations. By 1983 there were over 150 university ombudsmen of various kinds. Unfortunately, some of them are executive officers appointed directly by the university president, while others are appointed or elected by students, and thus often become advocates for either the administration or the students, rather than independent judges of fairness. The ombudsman idea has spread so far afield that in 1966 the president of the Michigan Bar Association appointed all seventeen past-presidents as "ombudsmen" to hear complaints from lawyers against officials of their own Association. The name ombudsman has even been given to complaint columns in newspapers, and to the person handling customers' problems in a San Francisco department store.

As this survey shows, a serious problem connected with implementing the ombudsman plan in the United States is how to preserve the precise meaning of the ombudsman concept. Other problems are how to prevent the ombudsman from becoming an arm of the executive, and how to keep him independent and non-partisan. Because of the strong tradition of executive and partisan appointment in the United States, special qualifications and procedures for his appointment are required if these problems are to be solved. Nevertheless, the new state and local offices in the United States have already developed a unique feature that is a significant improvement over plans elsewhere: the simple expedient of allowing and encouraging complaints to be initiated by telephone.

Footnotes - Chapter Ten

1.   William Cahn, <u>Report on the Ombudsman</u> (Mineola, N.Y., November 1966), pp. 28 (mimeo).

11.

THE CASE FOR THE PLAN
IN CANADA

Canada's federal and provincial governments share the general characteristics of the parliamentary system that exists in Commonwealth countries. Among its main features are: a union of executive and legislative powers in a politically dominant cabinet; a single-member, single-vote electoral system that often throws up a huge parliamentary majority which gives obedient support to that cabinet; a tradition of secrecy that permeates the whole administrative structure; and severely limited opportunities for the appeal or judicial review of administrative decisions. All of these lend support to the proposition that the citizens and parliament need the help of an ombudsman in any attempt to get at the facts regarding a complaint of maladministration or arbitrary administrative action.

In fact, there is a greater need for the ombudsman institution in Canada than in the United States or some of the other Commonwealth countries. Though a Charter of Rights was included in Canada's revised constitution of 1982, these rights can be overriden by an ordinary law of parliament or a provincial legislature. Unlike the United Kingdom, Canada has only a few administrative tribunals, where decisions can be made in a judicial manner, and no Council on Administrative Tribunals. Canada's political system also has the following weaknesses: inadequate legislative prescription of administrative procedure; many regulatory boards and commissions with power to decide cases but few provisions for appeal to the courts; antiquated laws on Crown privilege, expropriation and liability; weak arrangements for free legal aid to needy citizens; and no formal procedures in either the central parliament or the provincial legislatures for settling the grievances of individuals. In addition to all this, the federal division of powers means that the provisions protecting the citizen's rights against administrative action are worse in some provinces than in others, and that the administration of justice varies because, though the federal government appoints and pays the judges, the provinces appoint all magistrates and control the organization and civil procedure of provincial and lower courts.

Present Inadequacies

Let us review some of these points more fully. First, only in rare cases has an administrative procedure been laid down by law for departments, boards or administrative tribunals to follow in dealing with individual cases. On the other hand, the United States has had a general Administrative Procedure Act for the federal administration since 1946, and most American states have such an act. Similar acts for federal and provincial administration in Canada have been proposed for several years by the Canadian Bar Association, but by mid-1982 only Alberta and Ontario had adopted a general, comprehensive Procedures Act. The governments of both Britain and the U.S. have had elaborate investigations of administrative procedure by official bodies, but in Canada little has been done about studying the problem, especially at the federal level. Moreover, Britain has created a Council on Administrative Tribunals to improve their procedures, while the federal government in the U.S has set up a similar body, the Administrative Conference of the United States.

In Canada the appeals available to a citizen in a case where he believes that an arbitrary decision has been made, or where he has some other grievance against official action or inaction, are very limited. True, both levels of government have set up some specialized appeal bodies, such as the federal Tax Appeal Board and the Immigration Appeal Board, and appeals from the federal bodies may be taken to the Federal Court, set up in 1970. But there is no comprehensive system of administrative appeal courts as in several countries of Western Europe, which have a complete network of courts covering all administrative actions. Besides the famous Conseil d'Etat in France, there is also an excellent system of administrative courts in West Germany. This had existed in Germany during the inter-war years, and its jurisdiction was greatly extended in West Germany under the 1949 constitution.

The opportunity for the ordinary courts to review administrative decisions is also seriously limited in Canada. At both levels of government there are laws providing for the creation of an administrative board or commission, which include a privative clause stating that there shall be no appeal from its decisions to the courts. Also, there are no general legislative provisions for court review, except in Ontario and British Columbia where Judicial Review Procedure Acts have been passed in recent years. Elsewhere, because review is based on the common law, the way in which cases are brought before the courts for review is very complicated. This is done by ancient writs, and often it takes a very skilled lawyer to know which kind of writ must be used; if he makes a mistake, the review may be refused. Hence, it may be difficult to get a decision before the courts for review.

Another serious limitation on court review is that the courts usually have taken the stand that they will make a decision on the law only, and an appeal on the merits of a case cannot be brought before them. Where legislation has granted a discretion to an official or body, the courts have wisely taken the stand that they should not substitute their lay judgment for that of the expert administrator. But they have tended to interpret the scope of this discretion much too broadly and do not even question whether the decision was reasonable.

Additional problems are that the courts operate very slowly and that their procedure is likely to be very costly in relation to the importance of the issue or the money involved. A citizen would therefore hesitate, especially in a minor case, to appeal an administrative grievance to the courts. Legal aid for the poor, which varies from province to province, is generally inadequate. Many other countries are far ahead of Canada in providing schemes of legal aid for people who cannot afford counsel to appear in the courts or to lodge appeals on their behalf. An example is the "store-front" lawyers that were provided for the poor by the federal Office of Economic Opportunity in the United States. Another is the 4,500 administrative counsellors in Japan (described in Professor Gellhorn's book, Ombudsmen and Others), whose job is to provide help to citizens in appealing against official action. An ombudsman would be of considerable help in this respect. He would not only provide legal advice in minor cases; he would also recommend legal aid where it is necessary to fight administrative cases in the courts, as the ombudsman has done in Denmark.

Finally, Canada is worse off than other Commonwealth countries in the opportunities available to citizens to air their grievances in parliament. Because of the breadth of the country, members cannot easily maintain contact with their constituents, as they can in Britain where many members on weekends hold "surgery hours" for giving advice and receiving complaints. As Professor Kersell has pointed out in his thorough study of parliamentary control:

Canadians and their representatives in parliament have no procedure for ventilating grievances which compares with Australian "Grievance Day," or for that matter, with British Question Time or New Zealand public petitions. There is no procedure in the Canadian House which in practice provides the back bench Member of Parliament with an adequate opportunity to air a constituent's bona fide grievance without first gaining the co-operation of his party in Parliament.[1]

If a grievance were to demand the attention of his whole parliamentary party, it would have to be a very serious one indeed. Even so, there is no parliamentary procedure for sifting evidence or making recommendations. Thus, under Canada's parliamentary system, involving the executive's dominance over the legislature and its tradition of secrecy, there is no easy way for cases of maladministration to come to light unless there is an ombudsman.

Before the first two provincial ombudsman plans were adopted in 1967, one of the most frequently voiced objections to the plan for either the federal or provincial governments was that it was not needed. It was said that citizens' rights were adequately protected already, and one didn't "hear about" very many cases of persons who had been dealt with unfairly by officials. The objectors did not appreciate that only some of the most serious cases were revealed and that, since such cases concerned isolated individuals, often they were not widely publicized by the press and were soon forgotten by the public.

Cases of Maladministration

To meet this objection, I made a point of collecting cases of maladministration, arbitrariness and outright injustice that had been publicly reported within the preceding decade. In all of them an ombudsman could have improved the situation for the complainant, usually by finding out the true facts at a much earlier date, by obtaining either redress or a change in the decision, and by doing so with far less injurious publicity than with a grievance aired in the legislature. In several cases he would no doubt have secured administrative and perhaps even legislative reforms.

These cases reveal a bewildering variety of bureaucratic bungling at all three levels of government - federal, provincial and local. They ranged from simple (but nonetheless serious) cases of red tape such as failure to answer an inquiry or make a decision, to heart-rending stories which were shocking enough to show that something had to be done. Examples from the 1950s are: the case in which a sane young man was incarcerated for three years, and others for shorter periods, in a Montreal prison madhouse amid unspeakable conditions of filth and squalor; the case of the Doukhobor children of British Columbia, who were hunted down by police and placed in "educational concentration camps" because their parents' religious beliefs prevented them from going to public schools.

The young man's case came to light only because an unofficial volunteer ombudsman, Jacques Hébert, wrote a book about it and persistently publicized his plight in a newspaper. The case of the Doukhobor children is one that graphically points up the need for ombudsmen in all provinces, because of the division of authority between the federal and provincial governments. The childrens' parents were admittedly breaking the province's school attendance law. The wrong lay in the harsh and inhuman manner in which the law was enforced by the province. Yet the federal government looked on from the sidelines, reluctant to act or even to comment because the case lay in the delicate area of provincial rights.

On the whole, Canada public servants are noted for their integrity. Yet many instances of abuse of office had been revealed at all levels of government during the decade before the first provincial adoptions in 1967. Typical examples were: the notorious case in which personnel at the military base in Petawawa, Ontario, organized a system for pilfering army materials on a large scale, and are even alleged to have put the names of horses on the payroll; a case in which a provincial cabinet minister in British Columbia accepted a bribe; and numerous cases at the municipal level in which civic officials used their offices for personal gain. Most of these cases came to light only through public agitation and special arrangements for investigation. Their detection would probably have come much sooner - and some may even have been prevented - had ombudsmen been on the scene.

All of the above examples were such serious caes that they were publicly revealed. But there were countless others of individual grievances that were never brought to light and in some of which the aggrieved person may have suffered years of heart-breaking frustration. This became clear after I wrote my first magazine article on the ombudsman and spoke on radio and television about the idea in 1961. I became a kind of unofficial ombudsman myself, and received complaints from aggrieved citizens all across Canada, some complete with frighteningly complicated documentation. They were of much the same type that ombudsmen received.

On the basis of the Scandinavian experience, I estimated that the total case-load for ombudsmen at both the provincial and federal levels of government in Canada might be about 7,000 per year, with perhaps 3,000 at the federal level. Even using the low Danish figure of about 10 per cent that require some kind of corrective action, this meant that the number of cases of unremedied injustice in Canada was at least 700 per year. However, these figures are doubtless far too low because of the earlier-mentioned inadequacy of Canada's protections against arbitrary administration. Also, the federal division of the country into two levels of government causes administrative conflict and delay, and creates confusion for the citizens, who are likely to complain to the wrong level of government at first, thus increasing the total case load at both levels. Another significant difference from the Scandinavian countries is Canada's higher level of immigration and the accompanying administrative problems of eligibility and admission and citizenship.

The Role of Members of Parliament

While opponents of a federal-level scheme may admit that most of an ombudsman's cases could not be handled by the courts in Canada, they frequently argue that in a single-member district it is the job of the member of parliament (MP) to handle such cases for his district. In effect, they say, Canada already has numerous ombudsmen at the federal level of government, to say nothing of the representatives at the lower levels. To investigate this argument - to find out how many and what kinds of complaints MPs receive, how they handle them and whether they think an ombudsman would help - Mr. Llambias sent a questionnaire to all members of the House of Commons in the spring of 1964, and received 80 replies. [2] Nine of these were refusals of information, of which two were from ministers who declined to express any opinion for fear that this might be interpreted as government policy. Although the remainder is probably a biased sample, in the sense that only the most interested and sympathetic MPs replied, it does reveal some interesting facts.

The MPs were asked to estimate "how many complaints about some aspect of governmental administration in relation to individuals" they received per month from constituents, and there was a surprising scatter in the replies. Thirty-six MPs estimated they had fewer than 10 complaints per month while twelve said they received more than 30, and two indicated that they were burdened with as many as 65. The difference in the number of complaints seems to depend mainly on the rural or urban character of the constituencies and their total populations, which at present vary tremendously. The average number of complaints received by the forty-four MPs who replied to this question was about 15. Extending this average to all MPs would mean that in total they receive an estimated 4,000 per month, or nearly 50,000 per year. Even if we assume that it was mainly the overburdened MPs that replied, and that an average for all MPs would be closer to 10 per month, this would still mean a total of 32,000 complaints per year. The replies indicate that a surprising number of complaints concern provincial or local government and even non-governmental bodies. Only about 70 per cent relate to federal departments or agencies, so that complaints of the latter type may total about 22,000 per year.

To a question on whether the complaints concern the personality of officials, the manner of proceeding or the substance of the action taken, there was considerable variation in the replies. However, most of the MPs thought that about 10 per cent concern personalities, 35 per cent the manner of proceeding, and that a majority are directed to the substance of the action. It is likely that many of the latter deal with the reasonableness of a decision or the effect of a law or policy. These matters an ombudsman would not ordinarily investigate. MPs would continue to handle such cases, as well as requests for help and information and demands for change in the laws or regulations.

When the MPs were asked to indentify the areas of governmental activity into which complaints mainly fell, they named 41 different areas, departments and agencies. However, there was a heavy concentration on certain areas. Decisions regarding pensions seemed to cause the most trouble, appearing in 20 questionnaires. The next most common areas of complaint were citizenship and immigration, income tax, health and welfare, unemployment insurance, and veterans' affairs.

Questions were also asked on the efficacy of the existing procedure for handling complaints. It is interesting that there was considerable disagreement about whether being on the government or opposition side of the House made a difference to the success of a complaint, although a majority of the MPs felt that it made no difference. Perhaps the reason for this disagreement, as one stated, is that being on either the government or opposition side has advantages and disadvantages. While access to information is easier for government MPs, they are reluctant to ask a minister a question in the House for fear of embarrassing the government. As one MP wrote, "No questions to the minister, as I am on the government side!" An opposition MP, on the other hand, is free to publicize a case and to press an attack on the floor of the House.

A crucial question was: "Do you ever handle complaints which are settled in a manner unsatisfactory to you and/or the complainant?" To this the great majority (55 out of 63) answered yes, and many said that half or more of their complaints were settled unsatisfactorily. Various reasons were given for the shortcomings of the existing system. One stated bluntly, "Insufficient time and secretarial assistance to deal with each complaint." Another felt that a basic inadequacy of the system was the "weakness of individual MPs who are unwilling to intercede on behalf of the constituents." A third believed that not all MPs had the "experience or training to deal with some of the issues which arise," while two MPs pointed out that in most cases they could only obtain information at second hand from the minister or civil servant, since they lacked access to the files.

The MPs were then requested to describe one or more typical cases, or cases in which they felt that the minister's explanation and/or the department's action was unsatisfactory. Although many MPs felt they could not take the time to do this, the others went to the trouble of presenting a great variety of interesting and sometimes shocking cases. While space does not permit an analysis of these cases here, it is clear that many of them would fall within the competence of an ombudsman.

To the final question, whether they thought that a Parliamentary Complaints Commissioner (Ombudsman) would be of help, 53 MPs answered yes, 13 said no, and two were doubtful. Of this sample of 68, the proportion in favour of an ombudsman exceeded three to one.

The results of this survey clearly demonstrate that the number of grievances against the federal level of administration is great, and that federal legislators need the help of an ombudsman. They are too overloaded with work, too inadequately equipped, and not expert enough to handle the kind of case with which an ombudsman should deal.

Applying the Plan to Canada

Let us now turn to the question of whether the ombudsman plan needs to be adjusted to fit Canada's particular conditions and whether it will meet the need. New Zealand led the way in working out the problem of adapting the plan to a Commonwealth parliamentary system. But New Zealand's scheme is of little help in telling us how the plan should be adjusted to fit a large federal country. While the plan may have required considerable change to fit British conditions, it does not seem to require major adjustment to suit Canada.

In the first place, Canada has a much smaller population than Britain. More important, because Canada has a federal division of powers, there can be eleven separate offices - one to look after complaints against federal administrative action, and the others to handle complaints against the ten provincial administrations. Fortunately, this circumstance has given Canada three advantages: she had had eleven chances of adopting the plan; she has eleven opportunities for developing a scheme well-fitted to her special needs; and the work load of the ombudsman for each government will be small enough to be manageable. Hence there is no danger of a single office that would become too big, impersonal and bureaucratic.

Yet the need for additional protections against arbitrary administrative action is now so great in Canada that other reforms will be needed if a federal ombudsman system is not to become overloaded. For instance, we need much simpler judicial remedies, and wider opportunities for appeal to the courts, especially on points of fair legal procedure. The existing use of ancient writs is archaic, inadequate and confusing. There should be federal and provincial laws providing one simple method for appealing administrative decisions to the courts on questions of law and procedure, and uniform provisions regarding which types of matters may and may not be appealed to the courts.

There should also be federal and provincial laws on administrative procedure. These laws would spell out in general terms, and protect, the elementary rights of an individual affected by administrative action. For example, they would require that, wherever possible, officials should give reasons for their decisions and should give a fair hearing to persons likely to be adversely affected by a decision, as in the American Administrative Procedure Act. Also, many more adminisrtative appeal bodies are needed. Court review is costly and mainly restricted to the question of whether an agency exceeded its power, rather than whether its decision was fair and reasonable. Hence, in the thousands of instances where officials make decisions on individual cases, many more opportunities are needed for their review. Indeed, perhaps what Canada needs is a complete system of administrative courts, as in France and West Germany.

Canada also needs a much better system of free legal aid. It is true that a few provinces have recently improved their provisions for legal aid. But this is far from meeting the need. As in Ontario, legal aid should be made available for actions intended to redress administrative wrongdoing. And the federal government should stimulate the provinces to develop an acceptable minimum standard of legal aid across Canada.

In addition, the legal liability of federal and provincial officials needs to be clarified and codified. In many cases, citizens cannot successfully claim damages for injurious official action, either because the law does not regard the wrong done as actionable, or because only the official is considered liable and the prospect of recovering full damages from him is doubtful. The state should assume full liability for paying damages or making restitution to persons who are wrongfully injured by administrative action. At the same time, officials should be required to indemnify the state to the extent of their ability, for amounts paid by the state on account of their wrongdoing. This would increase their feeling of responsibility.

Furthermore, the rule of administrative secrecy should be reversed. Instead of the old rule that all administrative information is to remain secret unless the government chooses to release it, the rule should be that all administrative documents are open to the public, except in special cases where there is reason for them to remain secret, as in the U.S and the Nordic countries. This rule has worked successfully in these countries for many years. The withholding of official information not only denies the right of a citizen to have access to the reasons for a decision against him. It is inconsistent with the principle of free and open discussion of public policy in a democracy.

Fortunately, Canada has been moving slowly to reverse the rule of secrecy. Laws declaring the principle of openness and providing a public right of access to administrative documents were passed for Nova Scotia in 1977, New Brunswick in 1978, and Newfoundland in 1980. Also, the federal and Quebec legislatures approved access laws in June 1982, to go into effect in 1983. No doubt all or most of the other provinces will have similar legislation before many years have passed.

Though other reforms such as this are also necessary, ombudsman schemes can help to bring them about. Many of the reforms are legally complicated and technical, and it is therefore difficult to create an informed public opinion about them. Yet a government does not easily submit to the limitations upon the free exercise of its own executive powers that such reforms imply. The ombudsman plan, on the other hand, is simple, easily understood, and has great popular appeal. The public discussion generated by the creation of ombudsman schemes, and later by the ombudsmen's own proposals, will stimulate the kind of technical reforms of the law that require a fully informed public to promote them, and will help to form a strong public opinion that will insist upon their adoption.

Footnotes - Chapter Eleven

1.   John E. Kersell, Parliamentary Supervision of Delegated Legislation (London, 1960), 149.

2.   Mr. Llambias has given a full analysis of the results of this questionnaire, and has also recounted many cases of maladministration, in his M.A. thesis, The Need for an Ombudsman System in Canada (Ottawa: Carleton University, 1964).

12

CANADA'S
PROVINCIAL OMBUDSMEN

One of the great advantages of federal government is that an experiment with a new idea or institutional form can be tried on a small scale in one of the states or provinces first. If it is successful there, it will then spread to the others and can safely be adopted by the central government.

In fact, in Canada some of the provinces have been far ahead of the central government with innovations in recent years, and many important governmental reforms have come about in this way. Nor does the credit go to any one province. Saskatchewan pioneered with experiments in program budgeting and collective bargaining for civil servants. Manitoba set up the first politically independent electoral boundaries commission, and Quebec the first comprehensive plan for the control and state subsidy of election expenses. Also, the reduction of the voting age to eighteen occurred first in the provinces. Ontario's precedent-setting legislation for the control and court review of administrative procedure will no doubt similarly spread to the other provinces and the federal level. It is not surprising, then, that the ombudsman plan has already been established in nine of Canada's ten provinces, even though it has not yet been adopted by the federal government.

Proposals and Adoptions

The history of the proposals for provincial ombudsmen in Canada is recounted fully in Stanley Anderson's monograph, Canadian Ombudsman Proposals (1966), and can only be touched upon here. After the publication of my first article on the subject in a popular national magazine, Maclean's (Jan. 1961), a number of provincial bar associations and legislative representatives became interested in the idea, and began making specific proposals to provincial governments. By the early spring of 1964, the governments of three provinces - Saskatchewan, Nova Scotia and New Brunswick - were sufficiently interested in the idea to announce that it would be investigated. And in May the government of Ontario appointed a royal commission of inquiry into civil rights, one of whose objectives was to explore the idea. This inquiry had risen out of a controversy stirred up by the Ontario government's ill-fated police bill, which would have given the Ontario Police Commission power to question any suspect in secret and to hold him in custody indefinitely if he refused to answer questions.

By the end of 1965 private members' bills had been introduced not only in the federal parliament but also in the legislatures of British Columbia and Ontario. In addition, the Alberta Bar Association had drafted a model bill for that province. The scheme had also been discussed in the legislatures of Saskatchewan, Manitoba, and Nova Scotia. This meant that by 1966 the ombudsman idea had been at least considered by all of the provincial governments except those in Newfoundland, Prince Edward Island, and Quebec.

After outlining these developments in detail, Professor Anderson's monograph goes on to give a very perceptive and useful analysis of the proposals that had been presented in the form of draft or private members' bills. Proposals are a far cry from adoption, however. And in Canada private members' bills are not as significant as they are in the United States. Under Canada's parliamentary system the important thing is to have the cabinet adopt and propose a measure. By giving such detailed consideration to private members' bills, Professor Anderson may not have fully realized the significance of their distinction from government bills.

The plain fact is that, after several years of discussion and numerous proposals from various sources at the time his monograph was published (November 1966) no government in Canada had publicly committed itself to creating an ombudsman. In fact, by that time interest in the proposal actually seemed to have flagged. Although a parliamentary committee had recommended the plan for the federal level in 1965, the subject was not even mentioned in the federal government's Speech from the Throne for 1966. Near the end of that year, I was half-seriously thinking of writing an article entitled, "Whatever Happened to the Ombudsman?"

Meanwhile, two events had occurred which were destined to revive the idea. The Labour Party in Britain and the Union Nationale in Quebec, both of which were committed to the idea, had been elected to office. Suddenly, at the end of 1966 the governments of Manitoba, Alberta and Quebec all announced that they intended to introduce the plan. In December 1966 the government of Manitoba issued a White Paper, Citizen's Remedies Code, which indicated that its proposed Legislative Commissioner for Administration would act only at the request of a member of the legislature, as in Britain

and in Congressman Reuss's American bill, and that his jurisdiction would extend to local government. Also, the government of Newfoundland had announced in its speech from the
throne that the ombudsman idea would be referred for study
to a select committee of the legislature. By this time,
then, the proposal had received some kind of formal consideration by either the government or the legislature of all
ten provinces.

In January 1967 the government of Alberta ran a large
advertisement in newspapers across Canada headed "Ombudsman,
Commissioner of the Legislature," seeking applications for
an appointment to be made before July 1, at a salary of
$20,000 per annum. The qualifications sought were "a sub
stantial record of formal education and related experience,
preferably in law and the social sciences." Alberta's ombudsman bill was given approval on March 30, and on April 7
it was announced that the new ombudsman had been chosen by a
committee of the legislature from among 230 applications,
and would take office in September 1967. Alberta's act, the
first to be adopted in North America, is based largely on
the New Zealand legislation.

At the end of April the government of New Brunswick suddenly introduced an ombudsman bill sponsored by the premier.
Before the end of May it had passed in the legislature. Like
Alberta's act, it is modelled on that of New Zealand. A few
weeks before the provincial election in October (in which
the Liberal government was returned), the ombudsman was appointed. Thus, by the end of 1967, Canada had two provincial
schemes in operation.

The governments of Quebec and Manitoba, however, delayed
the introduction of their plans, and it appeared as though
the first ombudsman in Quebec might be created at the municipal rather than the provincial level, in the newly-created
city of Laval, which combined 14 former municipalities on
Jesus Island and is now the second largest city in Quebec.
The victorious civic party in Laval's first election had
included an ombudsman plank in its campaign platform, and
proposed to present a bill to the Quebec legislature establishing the office for Laval. Also, in January 1967 the
Lemay Commission in Quebec proposed the office as part of
its recommendation for a new regional government to encom-
pass the suburbs opposite Montreal's south shore. These
proposals did not come to fruition, however, and in 1968 the
provincial government's plan, which was essentially the same
as the schemes in Alberta and New Brunswick, was approved by
the legislature. Meanwhile, the government in Manitoba had
been defeated in an upset election by the New Democratic

party. However, the new government was enthusiastic about the ombudsman idea, and immediately introduced a revised bill, which was adopted in 1969. The most important revision was to remove the provision in the original proposal requiring complaints to go first to a member of the legislature.

Two more provincial plans were approved in 1970, in Nova Scotia and Newfoundland. Nova Scotia's ombudsman was appointed early in 1971, but Newfoundland's law had not been proclaimed by the date of the government's defeat in October 1971, and the new Conservative government was in no hurry to implement the plan. Also, in 1971 a New Democratic government had come into power in Saskatchewan with the plan as part of its platform, and an ombudsman act was approved early in 1972. As in Alberta, the position was advertised in the press, but the ombudsman was not appointed until after the end of the year. Thus, by 1973, six of Canada's ten provinces had ombudsman schemes in operation.

Ombudsman schemes went into effect in three more provinces before the end of the decade. Newfoundland's act was amended and implemented in 1975, and in that year Ontario, the most populous province, adopted the plan. With the creation of a scheme for British Columbia in 1979, Prince Edward Island, which may have a population too small to support a full-time ombudsman, remains the only province without an ombudsman plan.

The Ombudsmen and Their Work

The provincial ombudsmen have been appointed from a wide variety of backgrounds. The first ombudsman for Alberta was George McLellan, the retired head of the federal Royal Canadian Mounted Police, who had had many years of experience as a police officer in Alberta. The first ombudsman for Manitoba, George Maltby, was formerly police chief of a suburb of Winnipeg. The first ombudsman for Quebec, called the public protector, was Louis Marceau, former dean of the school of law at Laval University. New Brunswick's first ombudsman, Ross Flemington, formerly had been president of Mount Alison University and before that was a chaplain in the army. The first ombudsman for Nova Scotia, Harry D. Smith, had been principal of King's College at Dalhousie University, and at the time of his appointment was a professor of French at Nova Scotia Teachers' College. Ontario's first ombudsman, Arthur Maloney, had been a well-known criminal lawyer in Toronto. Both he and the first ombudsman in Newfoundland, Ambrose Peddle, were former politicians, both having been members of the Canadian House of Commons, while the first one in British Columbia, Karl Friedmann, had

been a professor of political science and had done considerable research on the ombudsman.

Traditionally the Scandinavian ombudsmen have been judges, and it is frequently stated that ombudsmen must have
legal training. Yet only one of the first provincial ombudsmen had any formal training in law. Their success indicates
that legal training is not essential provided that the ombudsman has a good legal advisor on his staff.

All of the provincial plans have common features based
on the New Zealand model. In each, the ombudsman is appointed for a term that does not coincide with that of the government, typically for four or five years (though for ten
years in New Brunswick, Newfoundland and Ontario), with the
possibility of reappointment. Like an auditor-general, he
is considered to be an officer of the legislature, and can
only be removed only by it. He is intended to be non-partisan and impartial, so that he is interested neither in embarrassing nor in protecting any particular party in power,
and can be trusted on all sides - by citizens, politicians
and civil servants. He receives complaints direct from the
public and has the power to investigate those that may be
justified. In order to protect civil servants from the publicity of unfair allegations, investigations are conducted
in private. If the ombudsman discovers an administrative error or abuse, he will request that remedial action be taken
by the department concerned. He has no power to enforce his
decisions, but he can publicize instances where action has
not been taken. Thus his key weapons are persuasion and publicity. An important aspect of his work is that he exoner-
ates civil servants in cases where unfair accusations have
been made, and thus supports the public's trust and confidence in the civil service.

Since the Canadian provinces vary greatly in population,
the number of complaints and enquiries received annually
varies greatly from province to province, ranging from about
500 in Newfoundland and Manitoba to nearly 10,000 in Ontario. A large proportion of them concern federal, private or
(in most provinces) municipal matters that are outside the
ombudsman's jurisdiction, but often he is able to direct the
complainant to a source of help.

Though the provincial plans are based on the New Zealand
model, and hence are very similar, there are some significant differences. Thus, while in most provinces the government has nominated the ombudsman, in some the legislature
has participated more actively in his appointment. For instance, in Alberta and British Columbia he was selected by a

committee of the legislature from a large number of applications after the position had been publicly advertised, and in Manitoba ombudsman Maltby's reappointment was made by a special all-party committee.

Another significant difference is that in Nova Scotia and New Brunswick the ombudsman's scope includes local government. In British Columbia the act provides for the inclusion of municipalities, regional districts, schools, universities, hospitals and the governing bodies of professional and occupational associations, but this part of the act had not been put into force by 1982.

As unusual feature of Ontario's plan is that a select committee of the legislature has been appointed to review the ombudsman's reports and to make general rules for his guidance. Ombudsman Maloney created considerable controversy over his large budgetary requests and staff, which grew to about 140. Ontario's scheme has two regional offices in Northern Ontario, while Quebec's has a regional office in Montreal.

Most of the provincial ombudsmen have the power to make special reports on important or urgent matters, but only a few of them have made much use of this power. The ombudsmen in Alberta and British Columbia, for instance, have issued a number of special reports.

A key feature of the office, like that of auditor-general, is the ombudsman's annual report to the legislature. Besides giving accounts of selected complaints and of his action on them, it makes recommendations for improving the civil service and amending unfair laws.

Anyone who has doubts about the value of the ombudsmen has only to read their accounts of some real grievances for which they have provided a remedy. For instance, Alberta's first ombudsman reported a case in which a man was beaten and robbed of $50. At the trial of his assailants the Crown tendered as evidence the man's money, which had been found on the assailants. After the trial the money was transferred to the provincial revenue fund rather than being returned to the man. Ombudsman McLellan's comment was: "I found it difficult to understand by what possible right the Crown wound up as the beneficiary of this criminal case, while the victim had the doleful satisfaction of seeing his assailants sentenced to penitentiary, while the Crown spent the proceeds of the robbery." As the omubdsman recommended, the money was finally returned to the victim.

Mr McLellan's second report revealed cases of many persons who had been found unfit to stand trial or found "not guilty" of criminal charges by reason of insanity, and who had been subsequently detained in a mental hospital by order of the provincial government. Some of these persons had been detained for periods of over twenty years, in one case twenty-seven years, without ever having had a review of their mental situation by an independent body. Successive governments were not even made aware that these people were being detained at the government's pleasure. As might be expected, he came to the conclusion that this situation was wrong and that their cases ought to be reviewed periodically.

A typical example of Ombudsman Flemington's work in New Brunswick was the case of a teacher who complained that she was unable to collect her pension when she wished to retire six months before the minimum age, after teaching for nearly thirty years. The regulations provided that she could not retire on pension unless she was either sixty or too infirm to work. Although physically sound, psychologically she felt unable to continue teaching. Dr. Flemington felt that the rules were too rigid and unfair in her case. As a result, on his recommendation she was granted a full pension and the regulations were reviewed by the government. Another example was his finding that the government's expropriation procedures did not give enough notice and information to landowners. On his recommendation, the government took steps to provide more notice and fuller explanations.

Among the cases investigated by Quebec's public protector during his first year in office was the discovery that a social welfare court order had kept an eighteen-year-old, mentally ill youth in prison for two years, although he had been convicted of no crime. The reason was that health department officials had neglected to admit him to a psychiatric hospital where he could receive help. Thanks to the intervention of Dr. Marceau, this negligence was rectified. Dr. Marceau also discovered that a complainant was still waiting for his final payment six years after his property had been expropriated by the government. As soon as the public protector looked into the matter, the long-standing balance was quickly paid.

During his first two years in office, Quebec's public protector became very visible to the Quebec public because of the importance of many of his cases. Early in 1969 he handled a complaint from an imprisoned F.L.Q. terrorist about his treatment by jail officials. Dr. Marceau found the complaint justified and remedial action was taken. At the time of the terrorist kidnappings in October 1970 he

113

again came into the news through his willingness to investigate the numerous complaints by people who were temporarily arrested under the War Measures Act for suspected or possible membership in the F.L.Q. On his recommendation, the Quebec government agreed to pay the innocent complainants for damages suffered as a result of the arrests.

The first report of Manitoba's ombudsman, like the reports of the three who had been in office longer, contained cases of administrative bungling, maladministration and delay. Typical of the many complaints of delay and inaction received by the ombudsmen is the complaint Mr. Maltby received from the author of an article submitted to Manitoba's Centennial Corporation for possible publication as part of the province's centennial celebration. The article had been in the hands of the corporation for about three months. During this time the author had made repeated unsuccessful calls in person and by telephone to find out what had happened to his manuscript. Two weeks previously he had written to the chairman of the corporation but had received no reply. Through Mr. Maltby's intervention the distressed complainant was finally granted a personal interview with the chairman of the corporation, thus largely satisfying his grievance over the delay and inaction.

Some Critical Comments

Though the provincial schemes have fitted easily into the parliamentary system and have been remarkably successful, let me conclude with some critical comments on their nature. The situation of provincial governments is quite different from that of a national government. Hence the provincial offices should not be mere carbon copies of national plans elsewhere. Because most provincial governments are relatively small, an ombudsman gets to know the senior officials personally and is less likely to criticize them. Also, the cabinet's control over the administration is more direct, party patronage exerts a greater influence, and provincial governments frequently have very large majorities in the legislatures for long periods of time. For these reasons, stronger provisions are needed to ensure the ombudsman's impartiality and independence from the executive. For instance, the law could require that he be nominated by a committee of the legislature and elected by a two-thirds majority of the legislature. If he is nominated by the government instead, this should be done in consultation with the leaders of the opposition parties. They should be asked for names, and the nomination should be approved by them. His budget should not come under the control of the executive's treasury board, and his staff should not be part of the provincial civil service.

Nor should the ombudsman's own salary be at the discretion of the executive. Although in most provincial schemes his salary is fixed in the legislation, the executive still has control over increases in his salary, and hence has an opportunity to punish him by a refusal of increases. Instead, increases should be made automatic by tying the salary to the level of that for a comparable office, as in New Brunswick, where it must be the same as that of a provincial supreme court judge.

A difference between the federal and provincial governments is that the latter control the municipalities. Hence there is a need for the provincial ombudsman to have jurisdiction over decisions made by municipal officials, as in Nova Scotia and New Brunswick. Also, at least the largest cities, such as Montreal, Toronto, Vancouver and Winnipeg, should have an ombudsman of their own, since a provincial ombudsman couldn't give them enough attention. Though there is a substantial number of city ombudsman plans in the United States, there has been no experimentation with such plans in Canada.

There is also a need for provincial ombudsmen to supervise the courts. While there may be grounds for exempting the higher courts from an ombudsman's supervision, the situation regarding the lower courts, which the provinces control completely, is different. The chief justice of the Supreme Court of Canada has some disciplinary control over the judges of the higher courts, but any disciplining of magistrates must be initiated by a provincial government. Because of the danger that the executive might interfere with judicial independence for political reasons, provincial governments don't often undertake to do this. Yet magistrates are often inadequately trained and inexperienced, and, because of the large volume of cases they must consider, frequently make decisions involving civil liberties that are too hasty; or they delay making decisions so long that the delay amounts to a denial of justice. Theoretically, the appeal system should take care of such faults, but it is in the lower courts that the real 'underdog' most frequently appears - with no education, no money, no counsel, and no thought of appeal. The case for including the lower courts in a provincial ombudsman scheme is therefore strong.

A final comment is that the provincial schemes are all copies of the New Zealand-Danish version, and are all much the same. The provinces should adopt improvements from elsewhere, such as initial complaints by collect telephone, and should experiment with other versions. It would be a valuable experiment, for instance, if one of them were to give its ombudsman supervision over the lower courts, or more specific powers to make unannounced inspections and to initiate investigations, as in Finland and Sweden, or were to add ombudsmen or an ombudsman for local government, as in Britain and New Zealand.

13.

A FEDERAL SCHEME
FOR CANADA

In 1963 and 1964 two startling cases of individual grievance against government administration shocked the public and promoted the idea of a federal ombudsman in Canada. The first was a case of bureaucratic bungling in which a seaman with an excellent record was discharged from the Royal Canadian Navy for no apparent reason. After much prodding from the opposition, the government finally revealed that he had been judged a security risk because of an allegation that his uncle had been a communist candidate in a recent federal election. Upon further investigation it proved to be a negligent case of mistaken identity: although the candidate had the same last name as the seaman, he was not the seaman's uncle!

In the second case (known as the "blood bomber" case), a man threw a milk carton of cow's blood from the gallery onto the floor of the House of Commons. It turned out that he was the head of "Underdog," an organization to help mistreated people. He had done this to dramatize the plight of a man with a grievance against the government: the man complained that he was wrongly suspected of being a communist because the Royal Canadian Mounted Police refused to acknowledge his earlier activities as an undercover agent for them, and he could find no way to have his case investigated. Two days later, in reply to a question in the House, the minister of justice stated that he was in favour of considering the idea of creating the office of ombudsman.

The reason for considering the idea was the realization that in the modern bureaucratic state there must be many cases of this kind that never come to light and so are never remedied. The office of ombudsman seemed eminently suited for investigating such cases. At the time of the seaman and "blood bomber" cases, the proposal for the office in Britain was being actively discussed.

Even before the revelation of these cases, the idea had received considerable publicity in Canada. Articles in learned journals and popular magazines had advocated ombudsmen for Canada at both the federal and provincial levels of government. Interest in the ombudsman proposal had been rising since New Zealand's adoption of the scheme in 1962. As early as December of that year, Arthur Smith, a member of the majority Conservative party, presented to the House of Commons a private member's bill for a parliamentary commissioner. As often happens with such bills, it was not debated or voted on. Much the same bill was introduced again in 1963, this time by R.N. Thompson, then leader of the Social Credit party, but its second reading was disallowed by the Speaker because a private member's bill may not propose an expenditure of public funds. He introduced it again as Bill C-7 in February 1964, with provision for the commission to be financed by private benefactions - an amendment obviously designed to circumvent the Speaker's previous ruling and not to be taken seriously. This time it was successfully debated. [1]

By then a royal commission had reported favourably on the idea [2] and a Liberal government was in power. Being more sympathetic to the proposal, the new government agreed to refer the bill to the House of Commons standing committee on privileges and elections. The committee took up the idea enthusiastically, and received evidence from expert witnesses, including Sir Guy Powles, the ombudsman for New Zealand. In February 1965 it recommended that the office be created, and in April 1965 the Pearson government announced that the ombudsman idea would be referred to a new royal commission being set up to study administrative bodies. Thus it appeared that a federal ombudsman plan was well on the way to being adopted.

The royal commission was never appointed, however, and no action was taken to implement the parliamentary committee's recommendation. Although the Trudeau government came to power in 1968 on the platform of a just society and participatory democracy, it mysteriously refused to adopt the plan.

Mr. Thompson deserves credit for keeping the subject alive in the federal parliament. He re-introduced his bill at each session for a decade, until his retirement from parliament. In later years he also presented a second bill containing a less far-reaching but also less effective proposal. This would give the ombudsman's functions to the auditor-general, who would be allowed to investigate only complaints received through members of parliament.

In view of the obvious success of the ombudsman plan elsewhere and at the provincial level, the Trudeau government's refusal to adopt it is strange. This is doubly so because the government provided a precedent for it and accepted the basic idea (though on a very limited scale) in the powers granted to the Commissioner of Official Languages, who was appointed in 1970 under the Official Languages Act of 1979. He is empowered to investigate complaints against federal offices for not dealing adequately with the public in both English and French. Like an ombudsman, he may also recommend remedies, and if they are not accepted, may report the matter to parliament. In his second year of operation he received about 1500 complaints. The number has remained high because he mounted a good publicity campaign and allowed complainants to call his office collect. In June 1972 he called together a historic two-day conference of Canadian ombudsmen, several of whom had not yet met. This was the first conference of ombudsmen ever held.

The few reasons that the Trudeau government has given for refusing to adopt a general ombudsman plan do not make much sense. In reply to a question in the House of Commons about the idea, the Prime Minister gave the silly answer that the Minister of Justice acts as the ombudsman. This shows a complete misconception of the office. Its main purpose is to provide an investigator who is completely independent of the ministers since they are the ones responsible for directing the civil service. Justice Minister Turner stated that the question of setting up the institution must wait until a detailed review had been conducted of administrative procedures and methods of appeal. Yet experience elsewhere has shown that, regardless of how good the procedures or avenues of appeal provided by the administration, an independent office standing outside the civil service is still needed as an instrument to build public trust in the bureaucracy. Also, it is a kind of overall umbrella to catch cases where no other adequate appeal procedures have been created.

Proposals for a Federal Scheme

The provincial ombudsmen have no power to review complaints against the thousands of administrative decisions that are made annually by federal civil servants. Yet, as we have seen, the need for the institution at the federal level is just as great as in the provinces and greater than in some other countries.

Clearly, the federal government needs a strong ombudsman institution with wide scope. What should be the nature of this office? What adjustments are needed to suit the central government of a relatively populous and far-flung federation such as Canada? As a basis for answering these questions, I shall analyze the provisions of Mr. Thompson's first bill, as a device for reaching conclusions about the main features of a workable federal scheme. This bill was introduced in

1972 as Bill C-52.[3] Like the provincial legislation, Bill C-52 was based on the New Zealand act of 1962, but it was a much simplified and condensed version.

An obvious point to note is that in Bill C-52 the ombudsman is called the parliamentary commissioner, and the word ombudsman does not appear. Yet it is a word that has by now become part of the English language, probably because it includes the word "man" at the end of it. It is significant that the first New Zealand bill did not use the word, but the second one included it in brackets in the title, after "parliamentary commissioner." This was done because of the rapid popular acceptance of the word; the parliamentary commissioner was constantly referred to in the press as an ombudsman, and he later referred to himself as the ombudsman. The term is also used in all provincial schemes except Quebec's, so there is no good reason for not adopting it. It has the advantage of being brief and intriguing, and it is specific in its connotations. The term parliamentary commissioner may mean any kind of office, and Quebec's "public protector" is also too sweeping, whereas the word ombudsman refers to a specific, limited scheme. We are lucky that the Swedish word for the office is not the same as the Finnish word: oikeusasiamies!

A serious problem under the parliamentary system is how the ombudsman should be appointed. Traditionally all appointments are made by the Crown, which in effect means the Prime Minister. Yet Canada has a party situation which is often quite different from that of Scandinavian countries. It has a long tradition of majority governments supported by a large majority in parliament. A serious danger here is that if the ombudsman is appointed by the chief executive he will be sympathetic or identified with the government of the day. In the Scandinavian countries, on the other hand, the ombudsman is appointed by the agreement of all political parties. Hence they are sure that he is independent of the government. Bill C-52 meets this problem fairly well by giving the parliamentary commissioner permanent tenure, and he can be removed only by parliament for cause. But provision should also be made for the opposition parties to agree on the appointment, to make sure that he has wide support and is independent. There is perhaps some danger that permanent tenure may make him feel too secure. In Scandinavia he is appointed for a limited period of only four years because it is accepted that each new parliament should be able to appoint its own officer, especially if it feels that the incumbent is not active enough, or that his powers are waning. But under the Canadian parliamentary system, in which the executive usually dominates the legislature, the need for his independence should override this consideration. He should be appointed either with permanent tenure or for a term longer than the life of a parliament.

Because of the weakness of other appeal mechanisms, the powers of an ombudsman in Canada should be very wide. His jurisdiction should include the army, public corporations, commissions, boards and agencies of all kinds. Bill C-52 sensibly gives very broad powers to the parliamentary commissioner. The scope of his jurisdiction would be even wider than that in New Zealand. The judiciary and the Governor General acting on the advice of the whole cabinet would be exempt from his purview, as in New Zealand, but any other "power or authority," apparently including individual ministers, could be investigated and criticized if need be. The author of the bill was obviously unimpressed by the fears expressed in Britain that an ombudsman might interfere with ministerial responsibility, for it included neither the proposal of the Whyatt Report that a minister should have power to stop an investigation or refuse to release departmental minutes, nor even the stipulation in New Zealand's act that, where an investigation relates to a recommendation made to a minister, the ombudsman must consult the minister at his request. Unlike the provisions in New Zealand, his powers of inquiry, rather than being spelled out in great detail, are simply said to be those of a commissioner under the Inquiries Act, and his investigations are not required to be private; no fee is required to make a complaint, no limits are placed on his power to investigate the armed services, and his scope is not limited to only those departments and agencies named in a schedule.

As in the New Zealand act, the parliamentary commissioner's grounds for criticizing an administrative action were to be very broad. For example, he could make recommendations where he adjudged that an authority or officer is administering a law "unreasonably, wrongly...or by using a discretionary power for an improper purpose, or on irrelevant grounds." Having the power to decide whether a federal power is being administered "wrongly" would give the ombudsman a very broad scope indeed. I am not sure that the legislation should go quite that far, because it would give the ombudsman the right to go into the merits or substance of decisions if he wished to do so. It would make the job far too big if he tried to review the merits of decisions, and is not his proper function anyway, except where he suspects that a real injustice has been done. I think the word "unreasonably" goes far enough in this direction, and that therefore the word "wrongly" is not needed.

Similarly, the statement of the commissioner's powers regarding publicity may be too broad. He is given virtually complete discretion in this regard. Under the bill, the commissioner could reveal the names of citizens and public servants involved in cases, and he could allow the press in on cases from the very beginning. In general, greater administrative openness is desirable, but he should not be empowered to reveal the names and details of a case until after his investigation is completed, except perhaps where a public accusation has been made and the air needs to be cleared by a public inquiry. Otherwise, the ombudsman could easily injure the reputation of a complainant, and could ruin that of a public servant by revealing an allegation against him which was later found to be unjustified. Most ombudsman laws therefore require secrecy until the investigation of a case is complete. On the other hand, publicity is one of the ombudsman's most powerful weapons. The rules governing the secrecy of his investigations and the publicity given to his decisions and recommendations must therefore be spelled out very carefully.

An important requirement needed to make the office effective is missing from Bill C-52. Provision should be made for one of the standing committees, or preferably a special committee, of the House of Commons to receive the ombudsman's annual report, consider it and hear his oral comments. This committee should look into cases where the administration has refused to follow his recommendations and should take up his proposals for legislative revision. If no such provision is made for parliamentary support to the ombudsman, the administration may not be called to account for refusing his recommendations.

Now for some more general comments on the nature of a federal scheme. Except for Britain and France, Canada is much bigger than any of the developed countries that now has a national legislative ombudsman, and so a single ombudsman at the federal level is likely to be overwhelmed with cases and unable to decide all of them personally. His office may become a cumbersome bureaucracy suffering from the same red tape and delay against which the citizens are making their complaints. In Britain and France, the main reason the ombudsman has not been overwhelmed with cases is that the number has been severely restricted by the requirement that he may take up only cases referred to him by members of parliament. But by the same token this restriction has seriously limited the effectiveness of the plan.

One obvious way of trying to meet this problem is to divide up the office, to set up several separate ombudsmen, each of whom would be responsible for a different area of government activity. One might be for the armed forces, one for the general area of social services, one for economic activities, and so on. Experience in countries having an ombudsman indicates that many complaints arise in the armed forces. The authoritarian nature of military organizations and the separate laws governing service personnel may be sufficiently different from civilian administration to justify a special military ombudsman for such complaints, as in Western Germany, Norway and Israel. In the United States an inspector general of the army performs a similar function, but he is not an independent officer of the legislature.

Except possibly for the armed forces, however, there are disadvantages to dividing up the office into separate ombudsmen for different activities. Often citizens would not know to which office they should complain. More serious would be the ombudsmen's lack of uniformity in the interpretation of their powers, in their treatment of cases, and especially in the rules of administrative procedure that they would develop. An important aspect of the single ombudsman office is that over the years it develops a body of administrative law, or set of fair procedural rules, that is applied uniformly and fairly by all government departments and agencies, so that a citizen is ensured of equal and just treatment by them all. This is especially important where, as at the federal level in Canada, there is no law on administrative procedures.

In order to allow an ombudsman to give personal attention to important cases even in a large country, and at the same time to avoid the disadvantages of dividing up the office, I have proposed instead that there should be a collegial commission, as mentioned earlier. All important complaints would be handled by at least one of the commissioners personally, and really serious cases would have the advantage of being considered by all of the commissioners, who would give a collective judgment carrying great weight.

The second time I was in Sweden, in 1962, I talked about this with Mr. Bexelius, then the civilian ombudsman. He had read my paper in which this proposal was originally made, and was rather intrigued by the idea. He called attention to the fact that Sweden, too, was a rather large country, and that the rapid advance of the welfare state in Sweden meant that the government's activities had grown rapidly. Though there was a deputy ombudsman who originally used to work only about six months a year, he had gradually come to work fulltime, but still could not provide enough assistance to the ombudsman. Mr. Bexelius thought that the ombudsman's work was now reaching the stage where he was unable to deal with all the complaints personally and at the same time engage in his important inspection activities as well. A few years later he made recommendations to the legislature for a reorganization of Sweden's ombudsman system. The extent to which he was influenced by this proposal for a commission is difficult to say, but it is interesting that in 1968 the legislature replaced his office and that of the ombudsman for military affairs by a joint body of ombudsmen who share their work. However, the Swedish ombudsmen do not decide important cases jointly, as a commission would.

The proposed ombudsman commission should travel about the country, either singly or as a group, in order to make its existence well known and to receive complaints orally, as the ombudsman has done in Ontario. This is now done by a number of national ombudsmen, including the three-man complaints commission in Austria. In addition regional offices should be set up in all large cities. Quebec's public protector set a world-wide precedent for this by opening a regional office in Montreal, while Israel's national plan now has three regional offices. Its easy accessibility helps to explain why it receives a relatively large number of complaints, about 7,000 a year.

A federal scheme for Canada should also receive initial complaints by telephone and be prepared to produce its own written version of these complaints. This would be of great convenience to complainants, especially those who are poor and illiterate. Hawaii's ombudsman has done this, and has found that about 70 per cent of his complaints are received by telephone, while about 20 per cent are through visits, and only about 10 per cent by mail. In contrast with the ombudsman in the early years of New Zealand's plan, who was required to charge a fee for each complaint, he even accepts complaints in the form of long-distance collect calls. As mentioned, Iowa's ombudsman and Canada's federal language commissioner now do this too. Imaginative features such as this are necessary if the office is to serve its maximum usefulness and reach all who are in need of its services.

Recent Developments

The second minister of justice under the Trudeau government, Mr. Otto Lang, seems to have taken the need for a federal plan more seriously than did Mr. Turner. Just before the election of October 30, 1972, he announced that within a year the government intended to create a commission for the protection of human rights that would include the functions of an ombudsman. But the other functions of the commission would have been incompatible with those of an ombudsman. Perhaps for this reason the proposal never came to fruition.

Instead, the government later sponsored the Canadian Human Rights Act, which was approved in 1977. The Act created an anti-discrimination commission and also provided protection and access to a person's own files held by the federal government. One of the commissioners is named as an ombudsman-like Privacy Commissioner, to investigate complaints from persons who have been refused access to their files. Like an ombudsman, the Privacy Comissioner was set up by law, only makes recommendations, and issues an annual report to be laid before parliament.

Meanwhile, the government had created the office of Correctional Investigator, to make recommendations on complaints from prisoners. This officer, however, is an executive ombudsman, appointed and reporting to the Solicitor General, as a commissioner under the Inquiries Act. The first appointment, made in 1973, was Ms Inger Hansen, who later became the first Privacy Commissioner.

Thus, by 1977 the federal government had created three ombudsman-like offices for special purposes, but had not yet adopted a general ombudsman plan. However, the Prime Minister had appointed a committee on the concept of the ombudsman, composed of senior officials, which reported favourably on the idea in 1977. And in 1978 the government introduced a bill modelled on the provincial plans.[4] But this bill lapsed when the Liberals lost the election in May 1979, and was not re-introduced when they regained power in 1980. Hence, by the end of 1982 Canada still had no general ombudsman at the federal level.

In 1982 the government added a fourth ombudsman-like office under its new law providing a general right of access to official records, the Information Commissioner. This officer is to make recommendations on complaints against refusals of requests for access to records, as the ombudsmen do in New Brunswick and Newfoundland. The new law also removed the Privacy Commissioner from the Canadian Human Rights Commission, and provided that the Privacy and Information Commissioners could be the same person.

There will certainly be a need to co-ordinate these two offices. If a general ombudsman scheme were to be adopted, their functions could be transferred to the ombudsman commission and they could become members of the commission. The functions of the Correctional Investigator could be similarly transferred. This co-ordination would create not only greater economy and efficiency, but also much more coherent and uniform decisions and interpretations of the law by all of these officers.

The new Conservative government under Prime Minister Brian Mulroney, which took office in 1984, has shown no interest in a comprehensive ombudsman plan. Yet, the need for and the success of such a plan have been amply demonstrated not only in other countries but also at the provincial level in Canada. Canada's provinces have been in the forefront of the spread of the institution from Scandinavia to the rest of the world. Indeed, the provincial plans in Canada have been so successful that they now serve as prototypes for other countries. Surely it is time for the federal government to create an even more successful version of the plan, so that Canada can be regarded as a model by the rest of the democratic world.

Footnotes - Chapter 13

1. Canada, <u>House of Commons Debates</u> 109, 21 (March 17, 1964), 1167-73.

2. Canada, Royal Commission on Government Organization, <u>Report</u> (Ottawa, 1963), Vol. 5, 94-5.

3. Bill C-52 was reprinted in the Appendix to the first edition of this book, <u>The Ombudsman Plan</u> (Toronto: McClelland and Stewart, 1973), now distributed by Carleton University Press, Ottawa.

4. For a detailed discussion of this bill, see Karl A. Friedmann and A.G. Milne, "The Federal Ombudsman Legislation: A Critique of Bill C-43," <u>Canadian Public Policy</u> VI, 1 (Winter 1980), 63-77.

Part Four:
The Worldwide Spread
Of The Idea

14.

HOW AND WHY
IT SPREAD

Considering the present worldwide interest in the ombudsman idea, it is strange that the system was not taken up by any country outside Sweden and Finland until after the second world war. What factors hindered and then promoted the international spread of the institution? Since it had existed in Sweden since 1809, and in Finland since 1919, it is remarkable that such closely related countries as Norway and Denmark did not become interested in it until after the war. Why did they not adopt it earlier, and why was it only later that the idea began to be widely discussed in other democratic countries?

The geographic position, cultural isolation and languages of Finland and Sweden were no doubt significant barriers to the spread of knowledge about the scheme. The idea for a military ombudsman in West Germany was originally proposed by a member of the federal legislature who had spent some time in Sweden as a refugee from Hitler. Other West Germans became interested because of their concern to create a democratic citizens' army. Probably the reasons a civil ombudsman has not yet been seriously considered there are that Western Germany has a well-developed system of administrative courts and petitions committees and that the office of military ombudsman has been controversial.

The geographic, linguistic and cultural isolation of the Nordic countries may have been somewhat a barrier to the earlier adoption of the system elsewhere, but this obstacle would not have been sufficient if social conditions elsewhere had called for it. This, I think, explains why Denmark and Norway, though having close linguistic and cultural ties with Sweden and Finland, did not adopt the institution until after the war, and also explains the peculiar circumstance that Norway and far-away New Zealand created the system in the same year, 1962. With the expansion of state activity during and after the war, with a new concern for protecting human rights, and with the growth of public education and participation, social conditions finally favoured the adoption of the plan.

At the same time, there is no doubt that some of the ombudsmen themselves have been very influential in bringing about the further spread of the institution, particularly Professor Hurwitz of Denmark, and then Judge Bexelius of Sweden and Sir Guy Powles of New Zealand, through their writing and speech-making foreign tours. All of them have had a great faith in the plan's efficacy and general applicability

Professor Hurwitz, for instance, after his appointment in 1955 as Denmark's first ombudsman, devoted much energy to promoting the plan. He wrote articles for European and international journals and travelled as far as Vienna to give speeches about it. He also willingly interrupted his busy schedule to give information to visitors or enquirers from other countries.

The early discussion of the plan in the English-speaking world and its adoption in New Zealand owes much to his ability and willingness to write and speak in English. He prepared a long pamphlet in English on his office, and wrote articles for British and American journals. He also spoke to academic audiences and appeared on television in Britain. Some indication of the strength of his impact there is that, after his return, he began to receive letters of complaint against British administration! In 1959, although he was not personally present, a paper of his was read and discussed at a United Nations seminar in Ceylon, which was attended by both the Attorney General and the Permanent Secretary for Justice of New Zealand. The paper was then pubished in a New Zealand journal, Political Science.

The idea for the scheme in New Zealand was promoted not only by this paper but also indirectly by Professor Hurwitz's stimulation of the discussion in Britain. New Zealand's ombudsman, Sir Guy Powles, was fond of saying that New Zealand's institution is a native one, noting that proposals for such an office had been made in New Zealand even before the Ceylon seminar, but lawyers and scholars in New Zealand no doubt followed the early discussion of the subject in British legal and other journals. It is significant that New Zealand's scheme is modelled closely on that of Denmark, and that in the final draft of the bill to create the office the term ombudsman was added as an alternative title.

The spread of the ombudsman idea has also been stimulated by the activities of the International Commission of Jurists and the United Nations. Both have taken an active interest in the idea, and both have organized periodic conferences on human rights in various parts of the world, at which the idea has been discussed. These conferences have included key officials from most of the countries in the area concerned. The International Commission of Jurists, in addition to the influential report prepared by its British Section in 1961, recommending a parliamentary commissioner for Britain, had frequent articles on the subject in its Bulletin. In 1965 its British Guyana Commission of Inquiry on Racial Problems in the Public Service recommended the scheme, and was thus partly responsible for its adoption in the new constitution of Guyana. In 1966 the Jurists held a colloquium in Ceylon on the rule of law, and it reported favourably on the plan for the Asian and Pacific region. In 1967 the U.N. held a similar seminar in Jamaica for Central and South America, with Ombudsman Bexelius as a guest expert. Also, the Council of Europe's Consultative Assembly passed a resolution in 1972 urging its members to adopt a version of the plan. As a result of such world-wide dis cussions, there have been ombudsman proposals and adoptions not only in the United States and Canada, but also in the United Kingdom, Australia, several countries of Western Europe, and many developing countries.

One of the strongest early arguments against the ombudsman was that the systems of government and law in Sweden and Finland were so distinct that the plan would not fit conditions in other countries. But its successful transfer to Denmark, Norway, and especially New Zealand, exploded this argument. New Zealand demonstrated that the plan could be successfully grafted onto the parliamentary system in a common-law country. On the other hand, all five of these countries were small in size and population, ranging from a population of well below three million in New Zealand to under eight million in Sweden. All five were also well-administered, developed democracies. There were therefore still doubts about how well it might work in populous, federal, racially heterogeneous, or developing countries.

Yet by the year 1967 - only five years after the adoptions in Norway and New Zealand - the spread of the ombudsman idea had gained such momentum that the plan had been adopted in five more countries: the United Kingdom, Guyana, Mauritius, the provinces of Alberta and New Brunswick in Canada, and the state of Hawaii in the USA. By the end of 1967, then, twelve legislative ombudsman plans were in existence: eight general plans at the national level, the specialized scheme for the armed services in West Germany, and the three plans for provincial or state governments in Canada and the United States. Except for Hawaii, the new adoptions were all in Commonwealth countries, and did not spread to others until later.

During the next fifteen years the plan spread very rapidly to other developed democracies and also to several developing countries. National legislative schemes have been established in such populous countries as France, Portugal, and Spain. The most populous jurisdiction to have adopted the plan is not a country but one of India's states, Uttar Pradesh (capital, Lucknow), which has a population of more than 110 million.

The ombudsman idea has spread to such an extent that by mid-1981, according to the annual survey of the International Omubdsman Institute, there were 75 general legislative ombudsman plans in 25 countries. Of these 75 plans, 19 were national, 34 were at the state or regional level, and 22 were local. Of the 25 countries, six had no national plan but had one or more plans at lower levels of government: Canada (9 provincial plans), India (4 state plans), Italy (4 regional), Switzerland (1 state, 1 local), United States (5 state, 13 local), West Germany (1 state). It is interesting that in the world's most decentralized federations one or more states have adopted the plan, while in two of these federations, Austria and Australia, there is also a plan at the national level.

Besides these general legislative plans, there were numerous specialized ombudsmen for particular purposes and general executive ombudsmen. The annual survey for 1980-81 lists about 80 specialized ombudsman offices, not counting over 150 university ombudsmen in North America. It also lists about 20 general executive ombudsman offices and about 120 other inquiry and complaint-handling offices on the executive side of government. Many of these were inspired or influenced by the ombudsman idea.

15.

DEVELOPED COUNTRIES

United Kingdom

Among the ombudsman developments outside North America, perhaps the most outstanding was the adoption in 1967 of a central plan for Great Britain, followed by separate plans for local government, regional health services, and Northern Ireland. In the fall of 1965, the new Labour government issued a White Paper setting forth the general principles of its proposed central plan for Great Britain.[1] It followed this up, in July 1966, by presenting its bill to parliament and announcing the appointment of Sir Edmund Compton, the retiring comptroller and auditor general, as Britain's first parliamentary commissioner for administration. This announcement was greeted with consternation by many members of parliament, not because of the person named - nearly all agreed that the choice was excellent - but because the appointment had been made by the government before the bill had been approved by parliament. However, the bill was approved in principle on October 18, Sir Edmund was granted funds for an office and staff on October 19, and the bill was referred to a standing committee for study. Incorporating amendments proposed by the standing committee, the bill was reported to parliament in November, was approved by parliament with further amendments in March, and Sir Edmund took office April 1, 1967, with about fifty assistants, all drawn from the civil service.

Compared with the systems established earlier, the British scheme places a number of serious limitations on the ombudsman's powers. The most important of these, stemming from the unnecessarily conservative proposals of the Whyatt report, are the provisions that complaints must be referred to him by members of Parliament and that he reports the results of the investigations to them rather than to the complainants. These provisions were made to reduce the load on the ombudsman in such a large country, and to make the scheme more palatable to members who feared loss of contact with their constituents. However, many people, including myself, feel that this is an undesirable restriction on the plan, because many complainants will not wish to take their case to a partisan politician, and he will be an extra screen between them and the administration. Also, a complainant should have the right to be a direct party in his own case. The latter point is met to some extent if, after a case has been referred to the commissioner, he is allowed to deal with the complainant directly.

A schedule to the Parliamentary Commissioner Act provides a list of the departments and authorities subject to investigation by the commissioner. Included are all ministries and departments and such agencies as the Civil Service Commission and the Central Office of Information. Another schedule, however, lists matters not subject to investigation. Among the most important of these are relations or dealings with foreign governments, security matters, police action, and personnel matters in the civil service and the armed forces. Also excluded are the public corporations, government contracts, local government, regional hospital boards, and the government of Northern Ireland.

Although the commissioner is appointed by the government, he holds office during good behaviour, can be removed only by parliament, and is expected to be an independent officer of parliament comparable to the comptroller and auditor general. He may have access to all departmental documents (including internal minutes) but not cabinet or cabinet committee papers. Ministers do not have the right of crown privilege to refuse the disclosure of documents, as they have in the courts, because the commissioner's investigations will be private. When they think it in "the public interest" however, they may instruct him to refrain from the subsequent publication of documents and information. Also, he is debarred from matters for which there are remedies in the courts. Since ministers can refuse to submit testimony to the courts, this has been criticized as intending to protect civil servants from embarrassing probings. On the other hand, a complaint can be made by a corporate body as well as an individual, and visitors from abroad are included among the possible complainants.

An important amendment to the revised bill, moved by the government, provided that the commissioner might not "review by way of appeal any decision taken by a government department or other authority in the exercise of a discretion." This amendment was attacked on the ground that it would emasculate the bill altogether by making it impossible for the commissioner to investigate any of the thousands of decisions where departments have a discretion. The government spokesman, however, claimed that the commissioner should not have the power to review the merits of a discretionary decision, and the amendment would not exclude him from reviewing the fairness of the method by which the decision was arrived at. Hoping to satisfy the criticism, the government later moved a substitute amendment in the House of Lords to say that he may not question the merits of a discretionary decision "taken without maladministration in the exercise of a discretion vested in any department or authority." This is still a far cry from New Zealand's legislation, which allows the ombudsman to review a decision if he thinks it is simply "wrong."

The limitations placed on the commissioner's scope and powers were greeted with a good deal of criticism by the press in Britain. He was amusingly described as a "muzzled watchdog," a "crusader without a sword," an "ombudsmanqué," and an "ombudsmouse." Because the "ombudsomissions" were so blatant, it was even suggested that the date he took office, April 1, was significant. Certainly Britain seems to have adopted the plan in an unnecessarily truncated form. It was argued that the commissioner's powers could be extended later, but the problem is that, once approved or created, a law or institution acquires a great deal of inertia which makes it difficult to change. In view of Labour's enthusiasm for a strong institution before it came to power, this case is a further illustration of a serious defect in the parliamentary system of government: because the executive proposes all important bills, and because it dominates the legislature, it is in a strong position to resist any provision that may limit its own powers. Scholars like J.D.B. Mitchell continue to argue that the need for fundamental reform of British public law is so great that the parliamentary commissioner is of little consequence. He handles only about 1,000 complaints a year, compared with about 7,000 received by Israel's complaints commissioner.

A good feature of the British scheme has been the establishment of a special committee of the House of Commons to consider the comissioner's reports. It has been very active and has made reports of its own to parliament. In recent years it has pressed for amendments to extend the commissioner's jurisdiction, notably to personnel matters in the public and armed services and to government contracts. But so far the government has refused to accept many of its recommendations.

The first proposal to create ombudsmen for local government was a bill presented by Lord Wade to the House of Lords [2] and given second reading in October 1966, the same month in which the government's parliamentary commissioner bill received its second reading in the House of Commons. It would have provided regional commissioners for administration, with powers to investigate complaints directly from the public against maladministration by local authorities in

England and Wales. After a brief debate and little public discussion, it was quickly defeated on the ground that the government had already declared its intention in the White Paper to consider eventually extending the parliamentary commissioner's powers to local government.

Then in 1969 a committee of Justice, the British section of the International Commission of Jurists, issued a report proposing a separate central office for local government, composed of five or six commissioners and a chief commissioner, who would receive complaints direct. However, in 1970 a White Paper, Reform of Local Government in England (Cmnd. 4276), instead proposed independent regional commissioners, and opposed direct access. The government then proceeded in 1974 with a plan of two commissions for local administration, one for England and one for Wales, with three regionally based local commissioners for England and one for Wales, appointed by the Secretary of State for the Environment. In each case the central parliamentary commissioner is also a member of the commission, though he does not undertake local investigations. Complaints must be in writing to a member of the local authority, and are then referred to the local commissioner. In 1975 a similar plan was set up for Scotland, with a single commissioner for local administration. The three commissions receive a total of about 2,700 referred complaints a year, nearly three times the number received by the parliamentary commissioner.

Instead of extending the powers of the parliamentary commissioner to the health services, the government created the office of health service commissioner under the National Health Service Act, for Scotland in 1972, and for England and Wales in 1973, and then in each case appointed the parliamentary commissioner to the post. Wearing these hats, he can receive complaints directly. As a result, he receives about 650 a year, and reports separately on them to parliament.

Meanwhile, legislation passed in 1969 had set up the office of parliamentary commissioner for Northern Ireland, to whom complaints were to be referred by a local member of the U.K. parliament, and the British commissioner had also been appointed to this post. In the same year the office of commissioner for complaints had also been established in Northern Ireland to receive complaints against local authorities and public bodies other than departments. Under this plan, complaints can be received directly. Since Sir Edmund Compton's retirement in 1971, the commissioner for complaints has also been appointed as parliamentary commissioner for Northern Ireland. As such, he has been receiving fewer than

150 referred complaints a year, while as commissioner for complaints he receives about 650 a year--a good illustration of the greater accessibility of an office that can receive complaints directly.   However, the number of complaints received against local authorities has been very small.   The Northern Ireland Act 1974 requires the reports of both offices to be laid before the U.K. parliament.

Australia

It is not surprising that Australia, with its close cultural ties to New Zealand, became interested in the ombudsman at an early date. Indeed, since Australia is a federation, the mystery is why the plan was not adopted earlier there at either the federal or state level. The explanation seems to be the dominance of the executive over the legislature in the Commonwealth parliamentary system. Although there were numerous proposals over a period of years, no government was willing to submit its own administration to inspection by an ombudsman until Western Australia adopted the plan late in 1971.

Regarding proposals made for the state level, in the case of Victoria they go back to October 1962, when the opposition leader returned from overseas convinced that Victoria should have an ombudsman. By October 1963 the government of Victoria had set up a parliamentary committee to look into the question but later allowed the inquiry to lapse. Other states in which the proposal had been actively discussed over a period of years were South Australia, New South Wales, Tasmania and Western Australia. In New South Wales, the government referred to idea to a Law Reform Commission, set up in 1966, and requested a draft bill.   In Western Australia, the first newspaper complaint column in Australia was begun in Perth's Daily News, in April 1965. In its first two years it received about 3,500 complaints, many of them against state and federal agencies. The column was actually called "The Ombudsman," and was influential in promoting the idea. [3]   The government of Tasmania was the first to sponsor an ombudsman bill. In 1970 this bill passed the state's lower house but was rejected by the upper house, and then an unfavourable government came into power.

Finally, the government of Western Australia sponsored a bill based on New Zealand's act, and it was approved in December 1971. A difference from New Zealand's act was that it extended to local government and to matters where there was already an appeal to a court or tribunal. The ombudsman, Oliver Dixon, who was formerly chief crown prosecutor, opened his office early in 1972, the first ombudsman in Australia.

The other states soon followed suit, all with legislation closely modelled on the New Zealand pattern. South Australia passed a law in 1972 that became effective in December of that year. Victoria adopted the plan in 1973, Queensland in 1974, and New South Wales also in 1974 but did not implement it until 1975. Thus five of the six states already had an ombudsman before legislation was passed at the federal level in 1976. The remaining state, Tasmania, finally passed an ombudsman act in 1979. Also, the Northern Territory approved a plan in 1977, and it became effective when the Territory was granted self-government in 1978. All of these plans, unlike most of the provincial ones in Canada, include local government.

At the federal level, both Prime Ministers Menzies and Holt had insisted that an ombudsman was unnecessary, but in 1971 the Commonwealth Administrative Review Committee recommended a General Counsel for Grievances who would be associated with a proposal Administrative Review Tribunal. Then the government, influenced by developments at the state level, sponsored the passage in 1976 of the Commonwealth Ombudsman Act, which provided for a federal ombudsman to be appointed by the government for a term of seven years. The first Commonwealth ombudsman, Jack Richardson, who took office in July 1977, had been a professor of law at the Australian National University in Canberra. Ombudsman Richardson is also a member of the Administrative Review Council, established in 1975 to advise the government on the reform of administrative procedure.

An interesting feature of the federal scheme is that the ombudsman has established regional offices in Sydney, Melbourne and Adelaide, and shares facilities with the state ombudsmen in Brisbane and Perth, including a joint telephone number. He has also delegated power to the Tasmanian ombudsman to investigate complaints in Tasmania against federal departments. Another interesting feature is that complaints and enquiries by telephone and in person have increased markedly in recent years. They jumped from about 500 in 1978-79 to over 11,000 in 1980-81, while the number of written complaints (about 2,800 in 1980-81) had increased only slightly. The state ombudsmen similarly receive a large number of informal complaints and enquiries. The number of written complaints each receives ranges from about 2,700 a year in New South Wales to about 600 (including federal matters) in Tasmania.

The Commonwealth ombudsman's scope was extended in 1981 to include the federal police, and under the Freedom of Information Act of 1982 includes complaints about refusal of

140

access to official documents. Also, the Minister of Defense announced in June 1981 that the office of Defence Force Ombudsman would be established, to be held by the Commonwealth ombudsman assisted by a Deputy Ombudsman (Defence Force).

Western Europe: National Plans

The continental European democracies, perhaps because the system of administrative courts in some of them partly met the need, did not at first take as much interest in the ombudsman plan as did the English-speaking world. Though their interest in the idea began in the early 1960's, no plan was actually adopted until after 1970, the first by a city in Switzerland (Zurich, in 1971). However, after France established a national plan in January 1973, new interest was taken in the idea, and a series of new adoptions began in Western Europe, notably national plans for Portugal (effective 1975), Austria (effective 1977), Netherlands (effective 1982), Ireland (adoption law 1980), and Spain (adoption law 1981), and an increasing number of regional plans in Italy, beginning in 1975. The states of Rhineland-Palatinate, West Germany, and Zurich, Switzerland, also established schemes in 1974 and 1978, respectively. Let us briefly review these recent developments in the countries of Western Europe.[4]

France

In the 1960s a few scholars had published articles about the ombudsman in French journals, but the first serious proposal was made in 1970 by Deputy Michel Poniatowski, who introduced a bill providing for a commissioner to be chosen for four years by members of the council of state and of the court of appeals. Support for the idea then rose steadily until the Aranda affair brought matters to a boil in the fall of 1972. M. Gabriel Aranda, a former public works official, claimed he had photocopied documents that implicated 48 public officials in scandals. During the ensuing controversy, President Pompidou conceded at a press conference over the affair on September 21 that something had to be done to make the administration accessible to the public. Then, early in October, Prime Minister Messmer announced that before the end of the year he would appoint an ombudsman-like commissioner to protect citizens against administrative abuse. The big Paris daily, Le Figaro, ran a name-finding contest for the new officer, and, with the help of members of the Academie Française as judges, came up with the name "Intercesseur." The government, however, adopted the name "Médiateur."

Because of the fear that the mediator might be overwhelmed with complaints, the government provided a built-in filter system like the one in Britain: complaints would have to be forwarded to him by members of parliament, either deputies or senators. Not unexpectedly, both the method of appointing the mediator and the public's inability to make direct complaints were criticized by proponents of the ombudsman plan. In January 1973, the new scheme was approved by the French parliament and Antoine Pinay, a popular former prime minister, was appointed to the post, at the age of 81. He was replaced in June 1974 by Aimé Paquet, a former mayor, deputy and minister, who in turn was replaced in 1980 by Robert Fabre, former leader of the small Radical party.

An unusual characteristic of the French plan is that all three mediators were former politicians. Symbolic of the political nature of the office is the fact that the mediator receives no pay. Mr. Paquet was so well known as a local politician in southeastern France that during his tenure a disproportionately large number of complaints came from that region. Mr. Fabre has retained his post as mayor of a small town in southern France, and two of his three senior staff were former active members of his political party. Though the former political reputations of the mediators have helped to publicize the office, their partisan history has probably inhibited many potential complainants. At the same time, the mediator is appointed for a definite term (six years, not renewable), and reports to parliament as well as to the President, so he is relatively independent of the government.

The French plan covers all levels of government, and another unusual feature is its decentralization through the use of a hundred local correspondents, one for each district (département) of France. Appointed by the mediator and serving without pay, they screen initial complaints and advise complainants on how to prepare and submit their complaints. However, because formal complaints must first go to members of parliament, the number received annually by the mediator has been relatively small, despite a recent increase to about 6,000. There seems little doubt that this restriction has prevented the plan from meeting a large part of the need for which it was designed.

In his annual reports the mediator he has made a large number of proposals for administrative and legislative reform, many of which have been adopted, including a law on public access to administrative documents, which was passed in 1978.

Despite early predictions that the office could not be fitted into the French system of administrative law, it has been operating successfully for a number of years. Indeed, the term "médiateur" has become so popular that it has been used for a number of similar offices, such as the executive ombudsman for Paris, who is appointed by the mayor. Mr. Fabre fears that it will lose its unique meaning, as the word ombudsman has in the United States, and that using it for offices of a different nature will only confuse the public.

Portugal

The office of ombudsman in Portugal, called Provedor de Justica, was provided for in Portugal's new democratic constitution, which came into effect in April 1976, and a law governing the office was approved in November 1977. However, the First Provisional Government had already approved the establishment of the office by a decree in April 1975. This decree provided for the appointment of the Provedor de Justica by the President of the Republic from three names submitted by the Prime Minister and the Minister of Justice. Colonel Costa Bras was appointed and took office as Portugal's first ombudsman in March 1976. The new constitution provides that future ombudsmen are to be elected by the legislature (for a four-year term renewable for a second term). Since Colonel Bras was soon appointed to the cabinet, Dr. José de Magalhaes Godinho, an eminent politician, was elected in October 1976 to replace him. He was succeeded in 1981 by Eudora Pamplona Corte-Real, a former justice of the supreme administrative court and president of the study commission for the code of administrative procedure.

Portugal's plan was heavily influenced by the Scandinavian model and, unlike that of France, provides for complaints to be made directly. But, in addition to investigating administrative complaints, the Provedor de Justica has been given two additional functions. He is a member of the Supreme Council of the Judiciary, which is concerned with the appointment, transfer and discipline of judges, and which is headed by the President of the Republic. He also makes recommendations on the constitutionality of laws, decrees and regulations. Those that were passed before the adoption of the new constitution are often called into question because they conflict with it. Hence this function is particularly important and time-consuming.

Partly because of these additional functions he has a total staff of about 50, and there is some danger of the office becoming overloaded. By the end of the first year there was a big backlog of cases, which has been difficult to reduce because the number of cases has been growing each year. The Provedor now handles about 4,500 cases a year, of which about 100 arise from his own initiative.

In comparison with ombudsman plans elsewhere, 4,500 cases per year is not a large number for a country of ten million people. This may be partly because the Provedor has had little time to publicize his services throughout the country. His annual reports reveal that a very large proportion of the complaints come from the Lisbon district. Hence there may be a need for the Provedor to make periodic tours or to open regional offices in order to receive complaints from other areas.

The scope of the Provedor's jurisdiction is broad, extending to the actions of ministers, public corporations and local governments. He also has the function of protecting human rights under the new constitution, which has a long list of human rights, including procedural rights, with a separate section on economic, social and cultural rights. For instance, he might consider a complaint against an industry that makes too much noise or causes a health hazard, or a complaint from a locality that it has not been provided with adequate medical or school facilities. These cases are difficult for the Provedor because they involve matters of policy.

Regarding the independence of the office, the Provedor's own salary and rights of employment are prescribed to be the same as those of a minister. He chooses his own staff and has an independent budget. He is also free to hire and supervise his office staff within the terms of the general law governing public employees. In view of the intense rivalry among the political parties in Portugal's new democratic state, it is of course essential that the ombudsman should be regarded as independent. Since the first ombudsman had been nominated by the government, it was fortunate that the second one could be elected so soon by the legislative assembly.

Unfortunately, the name of the office, Protector of Justice, is somewhat misleading. If it leads the public to expect accomplishments of which the Provedor is incapable, it may result in some disillusionment with the institution in Portugal. Since the word ombudsman indicates more clearly the unique and specialized nature of the office, it is a pity that it has not yet come into popular usage in Portugal. Perhaps the Provedor could himself promote the use of the word ombudsman for his office, as the Parliamentary Commissioner did successfully in New Zealand.

Austria

Discussion of the ombudsman idea appears to have begun in Austria with the publication of an article on the subject as early as 1961, about the same time that the idea began to be discussed in many other countries. It was given a further boost when the Danish ombudsman was invited to make a speech in Vienna in 1963. The Austrian government accepted the idea in 1971, and in that year issued proposals for a constitutional amendment creating an office of three members nominated by the three largest political parties and elected by parliament. Six years later the Austrian parliament passed a constitutional law, which went into operation in July 1977, providing for a Volksanwaltschaft, which may be translated as the office of the People's Advocate. This office is based on the classical ombudsman model, except that it followed the earlier proposal that the office should have three ombudsmen, one named by each party. Dr. Franz Bauer was nominated by the Christian Democrats, Robert Weisz by the Socialist party, and Gustav Zeillinger by the Liberals, and all three were then elected by the legislature. Thus, like Sweden, Austria has a system of multiple ombudsmen. Unlike in Sweden, however, the ombudsmen act jointly as a collegial board or commission on important cases.

Other unusual characteristics of the Austrian plan are that the ombudsmen may initiate proceedings before the Constitutional Court to examine the legality of federal decrees, and that the state legislatures may vote to have the federal plan apply to state administration. There are precedents for the states agreeing to make use of federal agencies. For instance, the states use the Federal Financial Control Authority. Two of the states, Salzburg and Vienna, which is by far the most populous state in the federation, entered the plan from the beginning. Some of the other seven states are likely to do so too, because the federal plan already covers state administration where the state acts as an agent of the federal government, and because some states are too small to have their own plan.

All three of the first ombudsmen were formerly members of parliament. Only one, G. Zeillinger, was a lawyer, but their senior assistants are all lawyers. Each ombudsman has appointed his own senior assistant and secretary, and a senior official is the office manager and secretary of the ombudsman board. The office has a total staff of about twenty.

As in Sweden, each ombudsman is responsible for a different area of administration, and one is responsible for each of the states that have joined the plan. Thus, Weisz was assigned cases for the state administration of Vienna, and Bauer for Salzburg. Unlike the ombudsmen in Sweden, the Austrian ombudsmen often act in unison as a board. They meet about once a week and each is chairman for a year. Though each ombudsman settles minor cases on his own, proposed decisions on all important cases are reported to the other ombudsmen and either of them can ask for a case to come before the full board. An ombudsman will try to settle a case informally by making a recommendation to the department concerned, but if it refuses the recommendation, a formal recommendation is made by the whole board, and the department has eight weeks in which to give a reply. All board recommendations and departmental replies, and the board's comment on these replies, are reported in the annual report to parliament. It can be seen that, though the ombudsmen had previous party affiliations, the effect of acting collegially as a board is to ensure that their decisions on important cases will be non-partisan and to assure the public of this.

Regarding the independence of the institution, the ombudsmen are appointed for six years and can be reappointed for a second term, and have the status of minister. The ombudsman board has independent powers over its own personnel and budget, although the budget is supervised by the Federal Financial Control Authority. Also, there is a committee of parliament, the Constitutional Committee, to which the board reports. The ombudsmen appear before this committee to explain and discuss their report, and the committee makes recommendations on their report to parliament.

The office handles about 6,000 complaints a year, but a large proportion of these are outside its jurisdiction, partly because its name, People's Advocate, implies a lawyer dispensing free legal aid of all kinds. However, in contrast with the situation in France and Portugal, the word ombudsman is well known and more widely used by the public and press than the official title, so this helps to clarify the nature of the office, as it does in other countries.

An unusual feature of the Austrian scheme is the use of an ombudsman board or commission. Much of the literature on the ombudsman lays stress on the need for a single ombudsman to "humanize" the office and give it a personal touch, and the majority of schemes throughout the world provide for a single ombudsman. However, the first plans were adopted in rather small countries where the ombudsman could deal personally with all cases, as Dr. Vontobel does in Zurich. The trend in recent years has been toward a system of multiple ombudsmen or ombudsman boards or commissions. Even Sweden, the originator of the plan, amended its system in 1976 to provide for four ombudsmen, and New Zealand added two additional ombudsmen in 1977. Other countries which have an ombudsman board or commission are Tanzania, Zambia, Nigeria and Papua New Guinea. One of the great advantages of multiple ombudsmen is that they can specialize on different aspects of the administration. Another is that they can make final decisions more quickly, because in a large office with a single ombudsman, all cases must be referred to him.

There is an important difference, however, between a system of multiple ombudsmen, such as exists in Sweden, and an ombudsman board. With multiple ombudsmen there may be a problem of a lack of coordination in their work and inconsistency in the conclusions that they reach, so that they do not build up a uniform jurisprudence in administrative law. The system in Austria combines the advantages of multiple ombudsmen with those of a single ombudsman because they can specialize and make decisions individually in minor cases but meet as a group and make joint decisions on important cases. In countries where party rivalries are intense, it is difficult to reach agreement on the appointment of a single ombudsman who is acceptable to all political parties and not suspected of being partisan. Austria's system of an ombudsman board enables each of the major parties to nominate an ombudsman who is acceptable to the other parties, while the board system ensures that they will have a uniform view on important cases. In many countries with a single ombudsman, he is in effect appointed by the governing party, and may not be prepared to take a strong stand against the government in an important case. A group of ombudsmen on a board, with one or more nominated by an opposition party, are more likely to be willing to take a strong stand and to be acceptable to all sectors of the public. For such a system to work successfully, however, the political parties must be willing to nominate eminent persons who are not too partisan in their views. The concept of an ombudsman board is particularly relevant to populous countries which may be considering the plan, because it is often argued that in such countries a single ombudsman would be overloaded with cases. This was a main reason why Britain and France decided on the device of limiting the ombudsman's cases to those coming through members of parliament. Yet such a device prevents the plan from meeting much of the need. [5]

Netherlands

In the Netherlands, which did not have administrative courts, an ombudsman was proposed for the city of Rotterdam as early as 1964, but at first rejected by its council. The same year, following a study of the Scandinavian plan by J.G. Steenbeek, a commission of the Society for Administrative Law recommended a general plan for the Netherlands, and included a draft bill in its report. This report was discussed at the Society's annual meeting in September 1964, and most of the speakers were in favour of the plan. The Dr. Wiardi Beckman Foundation (the research arm of the Labour Party) also reported favourably on the idea. Since the government took no immediate action, in 1967 the commission for petitions of the two chambers of parliament proposed that it should be given the same powers as a parliamentary commission of inquiry to inspect documents and to hear public officials, and that an office should be set up to prepare the reports of the two committees.

In the 1968-69 session, however, the Ministers of Interior and Justice issued an "ombudsman memorandum" proposing an institution modelled on that of Denmark and Britain, but with more limited independence and power. Complaints would be routed through the commission for petitions, and the ombudsman would handle only those specifically authorized by the commission. Members of parliament have criticized these limitations, however, and the proposal was not adopted.

Then, in October 1976 the government submitted a plan in the form of a bill to the Lower House, but the House raised certain objections to it. After a change of government, the new Ministers of Home Affairs and Justice submitted a radically amended version in January 1980, a parliamentary committee produced a report on the new version in May, and a National Ombudsman Act was approved in February 1981, to become effective at the beginning of 1982. The first national ombudsman, appointed by the Lower House in September 1981, is Dr. J.F. Rang, a former professor of labour law at the University of Utrecht. His scope included only the central administration at first, but was expected to be extended to the provincial and local authorities before 1984. Rotterdam and the Hague set up their own local systems in 1978 and 1980, respectively.

Factors that have delayed the plan in the Netherlands are the existence of an active parliamentary committee on petitions, an extension of the scope of administrative appeal in 1976 through the creation of an independent judicial division of the Council of State, and the appearance in 1971 of a non-governmental television ombudsman, on which the more recent ones in Austria and Canada were modelled, who has remedied many complaints against the administration.

Ireland

Ireland took an early interest in the idea, but no official proposal was made until the Public Service Organization Review Group, appointed by the Minister of Finance, recommended the plan in 1969. Official interest then lapsed until parliament passed a private member's motion favouring an ombudsman in May 1975. An all-party committee chaired by the Minister of Finance then recommended a plan in May 1977, but the government changed in July and the new Minister decided to place a notice in the newspapers in January 1978 inviting public comments on the proposal. Finally, in November 1979, the government introduced a bill that became the Ombudsman Act in July 1980.

In its main features this Act follows the classical pattern. Initially it applies only to government departments, but is expected to be extended to local authorities, health boards and other bodies within three months of the ombudsman's appointment, which is to be made by the government in consultation with the leaders of the main opposition parties and with the approval of parliament. The appointment was delayed by the election in May 1981, but the new government was expected to appoint an ombudsman in 1983.

Spain

A national plan has also been implemented recently in Spain. Spain had made provision for a Defender of the People in its new democratic constitution, which became effective in December 1978. The wording in Article 54 is as follows:

An organic law shall regulate the institution of Defender of the People, who shall be the supreme instrument of the Cortes Generales, appointed by them to defend the rights contained in this Title; for this purpose he may supervise administrative activities, reporting thereon to the Cortes Generales.

Although this wording could provide an officer with functions to protect human rights that are much broader than those of an ombudsman, the organic law has instituted a version of the ombudsman plan.

My edited book, The Ombudsman: Citizen's Defender [6] had been translated into Spanish in 1973,[7] and then Spanish scholars produced books and articles on the subject.[8] In July 1979 the Spanish television program, "La Clave," devoted a program in prime time on a Saturday night to a panel discussion of the plan, and included as guest participants the chief ombudsman for Sweden, the ombudsman from Britain, two Spanish scholars, the head of a Spanish consumer organization, and myself. In October of that year the Spanish government accepted for parliamentary consideration an ombudsman bill drafted by Professor A. Gil Robles and presented by the opposition PSOE party. This bill follows the Swedish-Danish model. The government proposed amendments based on the British-French model, but these were not accepted. The final organic law was passed by the Cortes in April 1981. Also, the 1979 statutes granting autonomy to Spain's northern regions provide for separate regional ombudsmen.

According to the organic law, the Defender of the People is elected by the Cortes for a five-year term. The Congress and the Senate appoint special committees which, at a joint session, choose the candidate(s) for the post. The election is by the Congress with ratification by the Senate. Two deputies are also to be appointed and ratified by these special committees. The office is to be independent, and the expenses of the office and its staff are to be charged to the budget of the Cortes.

The Defender of the People may investigate the acts of all administrative authorities, even ministers. He may act on a complaint, on referral from members of the Congress and the Senate or on his own motion. Should an emergency be declared, he is to continue to exercise his powers. He may refer a matter to the Constitutional Court, and besides an annual report may make special reports to the Cortes. As can be seen, the Spanish plan closely follows the classical model. The first "Defender of the People" is Joaquin Ruiz Jimenez, a leading defender of human rights and a former minister of education.

Western Europe: Local, State and Regional Plans

Switzerland

The ombudsman idea has been discussed in Switzerland since 1960, when the Danish ombudsman made a speech in Berne at the invitation of the Swiss Society for the Rule of Law and Individual Freedom. The chairman of the Society subsequently published a paper proposing that the system should be introduced at the federal level by an amendment to the Swiss constitution, and in 1962 a commission of the Society proposed the appointment of both civil and military ombudsmen. In 1964 a Swiss scholar, Dr. Walter Haller, produced a book in German on the Swedish ombudsman, [9] and since then he has been one of the leading advocates of the idea.

Partly through his influence, provision was made for an ombudsman in a revision of Zurich's city charter, which was approved by the voters in 1970. The city council elected Dr. Jacques Vontobel, an eminent judge with experience in politics and administration, to take office in November 1971, and has re-elected him for a third four-year term. The office has most of the characteristics of a standard ombudsman plan, except for the lack of power to initiate investigations. Dr. Vontobel provides an additional human touch by personally interviewing most of his complainants. He has reported a rather small number of complaints received annually (about 400 a year), but the population of the city is only about 400,000, and he reports only those dealing with city matters. As with other plans at a lower level of government, quite a few of the complaints have been outside his scope because they deal with a higher level, but he has managed to take effective action on many of them.[10]

Largely because of the success of the plan in the city of Zurich, a proposal for an ombudsman for the canton (state) of Zurich was included in a referendum and approved in September 1977, by a vote of 234,268 in favour and 85,666 opposed. Thus Zurich became the first canton in Switzerland to have an ombudsman. According to Swiss constitutional law, a referendum is decisive, and a favourable vote means that its provisions automatically become law. For this reason, there was a strong "pro and con" press campaign at the time of the referendum, and this of course increased the public's knowledge of the office before it was even created.

The cantonal minister of justice had favoured a strong plan, but the government was split on the issue. Some ministers wanted only an "ombudsmouse," but a cantonal parliamentary committee strengthened the draft law before it was submitted in the referendum. The parliamentary committee also added a provision that the ombudsman could use his own initiative in investigating cases.

The first ombudsman, Dr. A. Wirth, was elected by the cantonal legislature in June 1978 and took office in September for a six-year term. He had been director of a section of the Federal Institute for Agricultural Research and also an active politician in the Christian People's party. He had also been chairman of the cantonal parliamentary committee that had revised the draft law. Since assuming office he has been receiving about 400 complaints a year, and has personally interviewed most of the complainants, thus indicating that he is following Dr. Vontobel's practice.

In view of the favourable reputation established for the office by Dr. Vontobel, and the prospective success of the similar office at the cantonal level, it is likely that additional cantons will now adopt the ombudsman plan. A committee of the Swiss council of cantonal governments has proposed that all large cantons (over 100,000 in population) should have an ombudsman.

The plan is also being actively discussed for the federal level. A motion favouring a federal scheme was presented to the Swiss Parliament as early as 1966 and in October 1977 the government issued a bill on the subject for discussion by the political parties and the cantons. The federal bill incorporates the main principles of a good plan. It provides for two equal ombudsmen and gives them strong, independent and comprehensive powers. However, it is in the form of an ordinary law, and some scholars, such as Walter Haller, argue that it should be a constitutional amendment in order to increase the office's independence. Since an amendment would require a popular vote, this would greatly increase public knowledge and understanding of the office. In 1969, because of financial constraints, the federal government decided to postpone introducing the bill until near the end of the legislative session in 1983.

West Germany

In 1974 Rhineland-Palatinate became the first state of West Germany to have an ombudsman. Because the federal government has had a military ombudsman since 1959, West Germany naturally took a serious interest in the idea of a general ombudsman when this idea began to spread internationally in the late 1960's. A society was formed to support the idea and unofficial proposals were made for the "city-states" of West Berlin, Bremen and Hamburg. The Hamburg proposal was in the form of a detailed draft bill modelled on the Danish plan, and was published in Mensch und Staat (No. 1, 1967), a journal of opinion which has strongly supported the ombudsman idea. In August 1967, Willi Weyer, then Minister of Interior for North-Rihne Westphalia, the largest state in the federation, proposed that the idea should be considered by the permanent Interstate Conference of Ministers of the Interior, and in September one of the most widely-read weeklies, Christ und Welt, published an article entitled, "When Will a West German Ombudsman Come?" The federal Minister of Justice at that time, Gustav Heinemann, said that he favoured a general plan for civil administration affairs, but felt that it should be tried out first in one or two of the smaller states.

After 1967 the enthusiasm for the idea declined. Rhineland-Palatinate eventually adopted a plan that went into operation in May 1974, but since then there have been no further adoptions, though West Berlin has an executive ombudsman appointed by the mayor.

The first ombudsman in Rhineland-Palatinate, Dr. Johannes Baptist Rossler, was president of the state assembly at the time of his appointment, and had chaired the assembly's petitions committee from 1965 to 1971. He was appointed for an eight-year term and can be reappointed. An unusual feature of the office is that the ombudsman also handles complaints that go to the petitions committee. Altogether he receives about 2,500 petitions and complaints a year, of which fewer than 100 are by telephone--an indication that the office emphasizes formal complaints.

Several factors help to explain why there have not been more adoptions to date in West Germany. One is the mixed reputation acquired by the military ombudsman due to the involvement of the first incumbents in public controversies. Another is West Germany's comprehensive system of administrative courts. And a third is the existence of active petitions committees in the federal legislature and all state legislatures except in Lower Saxony. Legislation passed in 1975 extended the powers of the Bundestag's petitions committee (a 27-person committee of the federal lower house) to investigate complaints against the federal administration. These powers include access to documents and the right to inspect and hold hearings. It now receives more than 11,000 requests and complaints a year, and the state committees receive more than 20,000. Hence, the most likely development in West Germany is that a version of the ombudsman plan will grow gradually out of the system of petitions committees, by providing them with a politically neutral senior officer to receive and investigate complaints on behalf of the committee.

Italy

The most important ombudsman development below the national level in Europe has been the recent rapid establishment of ombudsman plans for the regional governments in Italy, beginning with Tuscany in 1975 and Liguria in 1977. The ombudsman idea had been discussed in Italy during the 1960's. Later, a comprehensive comparative study published in 1974 by a group of scholars based at the University of Turin, was influential in promoting the idea.[11] However, it was not until the regional governments that had been promised in Italy's post-war constitution were finally created throughout the country in the 1970s that the idea came to fruition. The organic statutes for three of the fifteen new regions provided for a "civic defender" - in Lazio, Tuscany and Liguria - but the office was at first established only in Tuscany and Liguria. Other regions quickly followed: Campania with a regional law in 1978, Umbria in 1979, Lombardy and Lazio in 1980, and Fruilia-Venezia Guilia, Puglia, Mache and Piedmont in 1981. Thus by 1982 ten Italian regions had adopted the plan. The offices for these regions follow the pattern for ombudsmen elsewhere, but their scope is restricted to the regional level and does not include national, provincial or local administration. They are therefore very limited experiments with the ombudsman institution in Italy. An outline of the oldest plan, which I was able to study in operation in 1978, will give the reader some idea of the nature of Italy's ombudsmen.

Tuscany is the region that includes the city of Florence. It has a population of about 3.5 million, while the population of Florence is about 500,000. It includes nine provinces and 281 local governments. The office of civic defender was established by regional law no. 8, passed in January 1974, but did not become effective until May 1975. Dr. Italo de Vito, a retired provincial prefect, was appointed as the first civic defender. He was required to be appointed by a two-thirds majority vote of the regional council, which has 50 members. The procedure followed was for the party leaders to agree on proposing his name, and the favourable vote was unanimous.

The civic defender is appointed for a five-year term, which is renewable only once. His salary is fixed at the same level as that of a regional councillor, and he has an independent budget. He has the usual powers of an ombudsman, except that, unlike the civic defender in Liguria, he does not have the formal power to initiate investigations on his own. But he manages to do so in any case, and the law may be amended in this repect to conform with that of Liguria.

Although he has been receiving complaints at the rate of about 1,200 a year, he has a total staff of only four persons. This is not surprising since the number of public employees working for the region is only about 2,200, and only about 30 per cent of the complaints deal directly with regional matters. The others are mainly concerned with local, provincial, and especially central administration. Although these are formally outside his jurisdiction, he manages to get favourable action on a great many of them. His proposals for remedial action on cases within his jurisdiction go directly to the department concerned or to the regional council, according to the case. There is no general control over his office by the regional council and no special committee of the council to consider his reports. The main problems in the complaints that he has received are administrative delay and the refusal of officials to reply to enquiries and requests.

In recent years the idea of a national plan has also been discussed. The Liberal party has proposed a plan at the national level, and a study on the ombudsman has been published by the secretariat of the chamber of deputies. However, the prospects for adoption depend heavily on the success of the ombudsmen at the regional level. The regional ombudsmen, in turn, face a number of difficulties which are likely to diminish their effectiveness. One is the very fact that they are unable to remedy the large number of non-regional complaints that come to them, and this is likely to diminish their prestige. Also, they suffer from a lack of visibility. Their efforts at publicity have not been very effective and they have not become known to the average Italian citizen in their regions. Fortunately these difficulties can be overcome. The first would be automatically solved if an ombudsman were created at the national level and if either their jurisdiction were extended to the provincial and local levels or separate ombudsmen were created for these levels.

Other factors likely to diminish the effectiveness of the office in Italy are not so easy to overcome. One is the politicization of administration and the influencing of administrative decisions by political pressure. Another is the existence of pockets of corruption in Italian administration. With these factors an ombudsman is not very well equipped to deal. Because of them, and of the intense rivalry among the political parties, it is extremely important that in the Italian situation the ombudsman institution should be politically neutral and independent. Even if a person is found who is acceptable to all political parties and who is in fact non-partisan, the highly politicized nature of Italian life means that some sectors of the public are still likely to regard him as under the influence of a particular political party or configuration of parties. For these reasons, many people will not entrust him with really serious complaints against the administration, or if they do, he is not likely to be able to take effective action. As one Italian professor expressed it to me, they may be willing to complain to an ombudsman about minor cases of delay or failure to respond, but in serious cases they will either seek a "fixer" in one of the political parties, or, if they are in search of administrative justice, will take their case to the administrative courts. The latter, though not speedy, can usually reach a decision within about six months, and are probably regarded as more independent than a regional ombudsman.

Despite these difficulties, the first regional plans were successful enough to foster clones in other regions. The first ombudsmen have been regarded by the political parties as reasonably neutral and objective, and the ombudsmen themselves seem determined to remain independent and free from political influence. If they succeed in establishing this as a fact with the public by taking a strong stand against the administration in deserving cases, and if they succeed in increasing their visibility by judicious publicity, the prospects for the spread of the ombudsman institution to the remaining regions and even to the central government appear to be good.

Belgium

Proposals for a national plan in Belgium have been made by several senators and deputies for a number of years. A private organization, the Commission for Justice and Peace, has been preparing a study on the feasibility of a national plan, and a commission has been preparing a bill based on a proposal supported by the leaders of several political parties. The proposal is for two ombudsmen, one for each linguistic region. Also, the Belgian city of Bruges has passed an ordinance providing for an ombudsman to be appointed by competitive examination. Exams were held in 1980 but no candidate qualified, so the strictness of the qualifications is under review, and no appointment had been made by mid-1983.

An Overview

This survey reveals that within the short span of only fifteen years the ombudsman plan has spread from Scandinavia and Britain throughout the rest of Western Europe. It has been adopted at some level of government in every country except Luxembourg. Counting the older plans in Scandinavia and Britain, general national plans have now been adopted in ten countries of Western Europe. Besides Luxembourg, the only countries without such a plan are Belgium, Germany, Italy and Switzerland. It may not be long before Switzerland approves one, and it is probable that the other four countries will eventually adopt a version of the plan at the national level.

Japan

Among the developed countries, the most recent to take an interest in the ombudsman has been Japan. Since the war Japan has had complaint bureaus in its cities and prefectures, and a national executive complaint system that is unique in its comprehensiveness, decentralization and accessl"l&lbtk¹² Bhe Administrative Inspection Bureau of the Administrative Management Agency (AMA) has attached to it over 4,500 local Administrative Counsellors. They are appointed by the Director General of the AMA, who is a minister of state, and they serve on a voluntary basis in cities, towns and villages through Japan. Their job is to assist the public in making requests, giving opinions or registering complaints regarding the national administration, and to forward genuine complaints to the Inspection Bureau, which also receives requests, opinions and complaint directly in some 40 district offices. The Bureau thus receives and acts on over 30,000 complaints a year. Some of the Counsellors also serve as Civil Liberties Commissioners, of which there are over 11,000, appointed by the Minister of Justice.

In recent years some Japanese scholars and others who have studied the ombudsman concept have become convinced that the complaint-handling function of the Inspection Bureau is not independent enough of the government. The AMA therefore set up a study group on the ombudsman. Its report, published in 1981, proposed that an independent ombudsman-like agency should be created to investigate complaints and seek remedies. This proposal was supported by the Provisional Commission on Administrative Reform when it reported on the matter near the end of 1982, and was to be further discussed at a conference held by the school of law in Chuo University in the fall of 1983.

According to the proposal, the new agency would be headed by three or more ombudsmen who would be appointed by the government with the consent of parliament, but the agency would be part of the executive branch. One therefore wonders whether it would be independent enough. The study group's main reason for not recommending that the agency should be attached to parliament may have been a fear of political interference in its work by MPs. Since the group concentrated much of its study on Britain and France, it may not have realized that the classical ombudsman institution elsewhere is independent of parliament except for matters of broad policy, and that MPs are not allowed to influence decisions on particular cases. If the proposed agency were to be made even more independent of the executive as an agency of parliament, and if the administrative counsellors were to become part of the new organization, Japan would then have the most decentralized and accessible ombudsman plan in the world.

Footnotes - Chapter Fifteen

1. The Parliamentary Commissioner for Administration, Cmnd. 2767 (London: H.M.S.O.).

2. Local Government (Rights of the Public) Bill [H.L.] (London: H.M.S.O., 6 July 1966).

3. Letter to the author from J.R. Davies, Assistant Chief of Reporting Staff, April 5, 1967.

4. For a fuller discussion of the plans in Portugal, Austria, Italy and Zürich, see my "The New Ombudsman Plans in Western Europe," International Review of Administrative Sciences XLVI, 2 (1980).

5. For a fuller discussion of the proposal for an ombudsman board for populous countries, see my "A Public Complaints Commission," Policy Options 3, 2 (March-April 1982), 33-35.

6. London: Allen and Unwin; Toronto: University of Toronto Press; and Stockholm: Norstedt; 2nd ed., 1968.

7. El Ombudsman: El defensor del ciudadano (Mexico, D.F.: Fondo de Cultura Económica, 1973), translated by Eduardo L. Suarez, with a foreword by Daniel Escalante.

8. For example, A. Gil-Robles y Gil-Delgado, El control parlamentario de la administración (el Ombudsman) (Madrid: Instituto de Estudios Administrativos, 1977), pp. 334, and El Defensor del pueblo (Madrid: Editorial Civitas, 1979), pp. 167; and Ismael E. Pitarch, "Estructura i funcions de l'ombudsman al dret comparat. Propostes per a la Generalitat de Catalunya," Administració Pública, n. 1 (Juny, 1978), 129-172.

9. Der schwedische Justitieombudsman (Zürich: Polygraphischer Verlag, 1964), pp. 320.

10. A doctoral dissertation on Zürich's city ombudsman is: Beat Keller, Der Ombudsmann der Stadt Zürich (University of Zürich).

11. Constantino Mortati, ed., L'Ombudsman (Il difensore civico), Studi di Diritto Pubblico Comparato III (Torino: Unione Tipografico-Editrice Torinese, 1974).

12. For a fuller, but dated, discussion of this system in English, see the chapter on Japan in Walter Gellhorn's _Ombudsmen and Others_ (see Bibliography). Also, the Administrative Inspection Bureau has issued two information booklets in English: _Administrative Counselling_ (1980, 11 pp.) and _Administrative Inspection and Administrative Counselling_ (1979, 19 pp.).

16

DEVELOPING COUNTRIES

Because the post-war newly independent nations were adopting new constitutions and searching for new democratic institutions, they took an early interest in the ombudsman idea, and it spread rapidly among the developing countries of the world. In Israel, for instance, the cities of Tel-Aviv and Jerusalem appointed complaint officers popularly styled ombudsmen, as early as 1966. The one in Tel-Aviv, however, is part of the executive. The ombudsman in Jerusalem, who is appointed by the city council, seems to be the first genuine city ombudsman in the world. Haifa followed by appointing an ombudsman in 1974.

Israel's State Comptroller

More important, the Israeli state comptroller gradually took on the functions of an ombudsman.[1] This development came naturally because the comptroller, an officer of the legislature with no direct control over the administration, had been given broad powers to audit not only financial propriety but also general legality, efficiency and morality. From the outset in 1950, the first state comptroller deemed it right to handle complaints from the public as an aid to his supervision of the administration. It was only gradually, however, that his complaint-handling function became widely known. As a result, the number of complaints rose steadily, from about 1,300 in 1961 to over 3,000 after 1966.

The increasing popularity of the ombudsman idea in Israel resulted in proposals that the complaint-handling function should be especially recognized either by creating a separate ombudsman or by making specific legal provision for this function in the comptroller's office. A special committee of the legislature was set up in 1965 to consider these questions, and finally reported in favour of the second alternative because the comptroller's office, like the Swedish ombudsmen, successfully combines complaint-handling with efficiency inspections and recommendations for administrative improvement. As a result, in 1971 the complaint-handling function was made explicit by an amendment to the state comptroller's law which named him also as public complaints commissioner. The next year the number of complaints jumped to about 10,000, the most received at that time by any ombudsman in the world.

The handling of complaints, which of course is only a small part of the comptroller's functions, is under the supervision of a senior officer, who co-operates with the legal adviser and the division in charge of inspecting the body against which the complaint is directed. The system has the advantage of making use of the large corps of experienced investigators and efficiency experts in the comptroller's office. The procedure for handling complaints is very much like that of the ombudsman schemes and has been influenced by them.

Since the new scheme excluded the armed services, in July 1972 an amendment to the military law, much like the one amending the state comptroller's law, provided for a military ombudsman to be appointed by the minister of defence but with the approval of a committee of the legislature. A former chief of staff was appointed and took office in November.

Israel's idea of turning the legislative auditor into an ombudsman deserves careful study by other countries. However, in few others has he been given such broad powers to inspect and supervise general administrative efficiency as Israel's state comptroller already possessed.

Early Plans Elsewhere

Other developing countries in which the ombudsman plan was adopted at an early date are Guyana, Mauritius and Fiji. These former British dependencies are small states with populations under a million. The British Guiana Independence Conference of November 1965 made provision for the plan in the constitution for the new state of Guyana,[2] and the first ombudsman, formerly the Director of Public Prosecutions, was appointed on the eve of independence in May 1966. The plan was also included by the 1965 Mauritius Constitutional Conference in the new constitution for an independent Mauritius.[3] The effective date of this constitution was delayed, however, until after an election in 1967. A provision in both countries is that the ombudsman is to be appointed by the government only after consultation with opposition leaders, and in Guyana he can be removed only for cause upon the recommendation of a special tribunal. Both countries have a racially mixed population, and in both cases it was thought that an ombudsman would be especially useful for investigating complaints of racial discrimination by officials. But Guyana's first ombudsman handled only about 150 complaints a year, and the present ombudsman receives only about 300. In Mauritius the enabling legislation was not passed until 1969, and a Swedish judge was appointed to the office in 1970, but soon resigned because of interference by the government. The office receives only about 150 complaints a year. The new constitution granting independence to Fiji provided for the office in 1970. A judge of the supreme court was appointed as ombudsman in 1972, and was re-appointed for a third four-year term in 1980. He receives about 400 complaints a year, not counting numerous enquiries by telephone and in person.

In January 1966, the Ceylon Colloquium on the Rule of Law, which was attended by about a hundred jurists from the Asian and Pacific region, recommended the institution for that region, and in April-May 1967 the United Nations held a seminar in Jamaica on human rights, with the Swedish civil ombudsman as a guest expert. [4] The Latin American delegates agreed that the institution would suit their conditions, and urged the U.N. to publicize it in Latin American countries. These recommendations added considerable weight to the idea of ombudsmen for developing countries. For instance, in July 1967 the Jamaican section of the International Commission of Jurists proposed the plan for Jamaica, and it was eventually adopted there in 1978.

In this early period it was also proposed for Hong Kong, Singapore, Malaysia and Pakistan. After Singapore's break with Malaysia, a constitutional commission for Singapore, headed by the Chief Justice, in December 1966 recommended constitutional provisions for an ombudsman much like those for Guyana and Mauritius. [5] The government of Singapore refused to accept the plan on the ground that there had been insufficient experience with it yet in Commonwealth countries. Similarly, the Malaysian government did not implement a proposal prepared for it in 1968 by Sir Guy Powles, and provision for the plan in the new constitution for Pakistan was not implemented.

An early executive complaint system that was strongly influenced by the New Zealand model should also be mentioned. In April 1965, Tanzania's One-Party State Commission recommended that a five-man commission be appointed "to enquire into allegations of abuse of power by officials of both Government and Party alike." Accordingly, an act was passed in March 1966 providing for a Permanent Commission of Enquiry. This Commission receives complaints direct from the public and has the power of access to government documents. However, its members are appointed by the President and its first chairman was a former minister. It reports only to the President, he may stop any investigation, and the results of important investigations may not be made public. During their first months in office the chairman and secretary visited both New Zealand and Israel. The commissioners also toured the country to publicize the scheme. As a result, they now receive over 3,000 complaints a year. Zambia, which is also a one-party state, set up a similar Commission for Investigations under a provision of its 1973 constitution.

India: The Federal Proposal

A strong push to the idea of ombudsmen for developing countries was given by the comprehensive ombudsman scheme proposed for India in 1966 by its federal Administrative Reforms Commission. The ombudsman idea had been discussed in India for several years before then, and proposals had been made at both the state and federal levels. As early as 1963, for instance, the institution had been proposed by an official commission for the state of Rajasthan. Several other states set up ombudsman-like vigilance commissions to deal mainly with the problem of corruption, but these commissions were appointed by and responsible to the executive. Early in 1966, however, the Punjab Administrative Reforms Commission recommended that "in order to increase the utility of the vigilance commission, it should be made independent of government or ministerial influence."[6]

At the federal level, a committee on the prevention of corruption had in 1964 recommended the creation of a Central Vigilance Commission, headed by a single commissioner and composed of three directorates: vigilance, central police, and general complaints and redress. The commissioner would be appointed for a six-year term and would have the same independence as the auditor general. His functions and powers would be somewhat like those of New Zealand's ombudsman, except that he would also inspect for corruption and could initiate a prosecution against an official if he were not satisfied with the action taken by the government on his recommendation.[7] The government, however, accepted only part of the committee's recommendations. It created a vigilance commission but did not make it independent of executive influence, and it rejected the proposal for a directorate of general complaints and redress. Instead, in January 1966, it appointed a Commissioner for Public Grievances in the Ministry of Home Affairs to supervise the handling of grievances and the work of new complaints officers in the ministries and departments, and to receive and review grievances himself. To the end of March 1967, he had received about 1,400 complaints, and had obtained remedial action on many of them. The Commissioner and the departmental officers, however, were part of the administration itself. In October 1966, the Administrative Reforms Commission, in a special interim report, therefore proposed a new scheme for independent, ombudsman-like complaint officers to handle both allegations of corruption and personal grievances, [8] and his office was abolished in July 1967.

The new proposal was unusual in that it would include both levels of government and at the same time divide the top from the lower levels of administration. There would be a sort of super-ombudsman (the lokpal) with jurisdiction over both federal and state ministers and secretaries, and also a lower order of ombudsman (the lokayukta), one for the federal government and one for each state, to cover the levels below the federal and state secretaries. These officers would all be appointed by the President of India. They would be answerable only to him and to the federal or state legislatures, and would be independent of the federal and state cabinets. The lokpal would be appointed on the advice of the prime minister, but only after he had consulted the chief justice and the leader of the opposition. A state lokayukta would be similarly appointed on the advice of a state's chief minister.

The Commission claimed that, though a constitutional revision would be desirable, the scheme could begin without such a revision. To an outside observer it is difficult to see how such a scheme could be effected in a federal system without a constitutional revision. It is also difficult to see how the super-ombudsman could be made answerable to both the federal and state legislatures, and how he and the sub-ombudsmen would be able to sort out their respective functions in a hierarchical system of administration for which ministers at the top are held responsible. However, the proposal represents an interesting attempt to divide up the heavy work of an ombudsman in a huge federal country. Evidence of the importance the government attached to the Commission's recommendations is that the first chairman, Morarji Desai, became deputy prime minister a few months after the interim report was issued.

Some of the states soon let it be known that they feared the supervision by the central government that such a scheme implied, however. As a result of their opposition, the central government accepted the proposal only for the federal level, and in 1968 introduced a bill to implement this part of the proposal. The bill provided for a lokpal and one or more lokayuktas whose work he would co-ordinate but who would decide cases at a lower level on their own, an

interesting arrangement designed to handle the heavy case-
load in a populous country more efficiently. By the fall of
1970 the bill had passed the lower house with amendments and
was before the upper house when parliament was dissolved.
The amended bill was reintroduced in August 1971, but the
government lost its enthusiasm for it and let it lapse.

No further action was taken on a national scheme until
the Janata government introduced an entirely new lokpal bill
in July 1977. This bill, however, departed far from the
ombudsman concept. It was for investigating allegations of
misconduct and corruption against ministers and members of
parliament rather than ordinary complaints against the
administration. In any case, the new Congress I government
under Indira Gandhi was not in favour of the bill, and it
too was allowed to lapse.

India: The State Ombudsmen

Meanwhile, ombudsman plans based on the proposals of the
Administrative Reforms Commission had been adopted by several of the states, though not all of these plans were implemented. The oldest state schemes are in Maharashtra and
Bihar, where they went into effect in 1972 and 1973, respectively. A scheme was adopted by Rajasthan in 1973, but it
can hardly be classed as a genuine ombudsman plan because it
is exclusively for serious allegations of misconduct or
corruption rather than ordinary administrative grievances.
In 1977 a scheme like those in Maharashtra and Bihar went
into effect in Uttar Pradesh. A similar plan was approved
for Madhya Pradesh in 1981, and in that year a bill for such
a plan was introduced in the legislature of Andhra Pradesh.
Thus, by 1982 ombudsman plans had been established in three
Indian states, two other states were in the process of adopting such plans, and an ombudsman-like plan was in operation
in Rajasthan.

Because of India's tremendous population, its state
plans cover larger populations than do any other legislative
plans in the world. Maharashtra and Bihar have populations
of over 60 million, while Uttar Pradesh has more than 110
million.

An unusual feature of Maharashtra's plan is the provision of two ombudsmen--a lokayukta for complaints against
ministers and permanent secretaries, and an upa-lokayukta
for complaints against officials below that level. The successive lokayuktas have been former high-court judges, while
the upa-lokayuktas have been former senior officials. In
practice the two ombudsmen share their work. Because there

are naturally far more complaints against lower officials, the lokayukta takes over a number of these cases.

Another unusual feature of the state plans has made them far less effective than they should be. Because of the great concern with political corruption in India, all of them are primarily directed at allegations of misconduct against officials and ministers. Fearful of exposure, the state governments have limited their ombudsmen's independence, powers and budgets, and have delayed laying their annual reports before the legislature, sometimes for years. Also, their complaint and investigation procedures are unnecessarily formal and elaborate, especially for minor complaints. Complainants are required to swear an affidavit, which costs time, trouble and usually money, and they can be imprisoned for a false declaration. Partly for these reasons, the state schemes meet only a fraction of the need and the number of complaints is very small. For instance, the office in Maharashtra registers only 1,500 to 2,000 a year.

Because the Indians had high hopes that the ombudsman system could be turned into an instrument to fight corruption, Indian scholars tend to regard the state plans as a failure. Yet the three schemes that have handled general administrative grievances have done much good work at remedying the kind of complaint with which an ombudsman ordinarily deals.

Recent Plans Elsewhere

In recent years several other developing countries in different parts of the world have adopted ombudsman plans, some so recently that they had not yet been established at the time of writing. Those in actual operation were in Papua New Guinea, Trinidad-Tobago, Ghana, the Solomon Islands and Bophuthatswana. Under the new constitution for Papua New Guinea, a three-person Ombudsman Commission was established in 1975. In the same year provision was made for an ombudsman in the new constitution for Trinidad-Tobago, and the scheme was implemented by an Ombudsman Act in 1977. Ghana's constitution of 1979 also provided for an ombudsman, to be appointed by the President acting in consultation with the Council of State, and with the approval of parliament. This provision was implemented by an Ombudsman Act, and an ombudsman was appointed in August 1980, but because of the military coup in 1981, the International Institute no longer classifies Ghana's plan as a legislative one. In the Solomon Islands, an Ombudsman Act was passed in 1980 and an ombudsman was appointed in 1982, while in Bophuthatswana a Control Commission (Ombudsman) Act was approved in 1980 and an ombudsman was appointed in 1981. In Barbados an Ombudsman Act was passed in 1980, but the Institute's survey reported that an ombudsman had not been appointed by mid-1983. In Saint Lucia the Constitution Order of 1978 provided for a parliamentary commissioner, and one was appointed in 1981.

Ombudsman-like complaint systems were also established in Nigeria in 1975 and in the Philippines in 1979. A Public Complaints Commission was set up in Nigeria by a decree of the military government in 1975, and the decree was incorporated into the Nigerian constitution of 1979, but Nigeria is again under military rule and the plan is not classified as a legislative one in the Institute's annual survey. The scheme covers not only federal, state and local government but also private companies. There are 20 commissioners--a chief commissioner and one in each state capital. They meet annually and issue a joint report with recommendations. In recent years they have received over 6,000 complaints a year.

The scheme in the Philippines dates back to a provision in the constitution of 1973 for an ombudsman office to be established by the National Assembly. This provision was implemented by a presidential decree in 1978 and went into operation in 1979. The ombudsman (called Tanodbayan) and four deputies for the three major island groups are appointed by the President for a seven-year non-renewable term. The office received nearly 4,000 complaints in its first year. Because the plan was implemented by decree and appointments are made by the President, it does not qualify as a legislative plan, and is no longer classified as one by the International Ombudsman Institute.

Provisions for legislative ombudsmen have also been included in the new or revised constitutions of several other developing countries, but had not been implemented by mid-1983. These countries include Bangladesh, where provision was made for the plan in the constitution of 1972, but an Ombudsman Act was not passed until 1980 and an ombudsman had not been appointed by mid-1983. The constitutions of Dominica (1978) and Zimbabwe have also provided for the plan.

In Sri Lanka, a Parliamentary Commissioner for Administration Act was approved in 1981, but the office has been classified by the Institute as an executive one. Complaints must first go to the Public Petitions Committee of the parliament, and the commissioner's decisions must be reported to the committee.

To sum up, by mid-1983 national schemes classified by the Institute as general legislative ombudsman offices were in operation in nine developing countries and had been recently adopted in two others, as compared with twelve national plans in operation and one recently adopted in the developed countries. Such offices were also in operation in three of India's most populous states and were being created in two others.

Special Problems

Influenced by all of these adoptions, other developing countries will no doubt take up the idea. The application of the plan to developing countries, however, has run into special problems. As I have already pointed out, the institution cannot cope with a situation where the administration is riddled with patronage or corruption, and it may fail if it is adopted in a truncated form, or in a form that subjects it to too much executive or partisan pressure. Unfortunately, in many developing countries the administration is riddled with patronage and corruption. And the need for rapid development has put a premium on a strong executive, which is not likely to endow an ombudsman with sufficient independence or powers of investigation, even where two or more political parties are allowed to exist. Where one party is dominant, as in India, the independence of an ombudsman will no doubt be limited. In a one-party state the ombudsman will almost inevitably be dominated by the executive.

Nevertheless, one-party states, like all states, have the problem of ensuring that minor bureaucrats in the field adhere to central policy and do not make decisions in accordance with their own personal whims or interests. For this reason, such states have an interest in one of the unique features of the ombudsman system, that of providing feedback from the people at the bottom of the administrative hierarchy to the politicians at the top. One-party states which do not have a Russian-style procurator are therefore likely to become interested in adopting a version of the ombudsman plan. However, this version will be a far cry from the original schemes. It will be an arm of the executive rather than the legislature, and will be more like an administrative control bureau than an independent investigator.

Although there are reasons for concluding that the ombudsman plan will not work as successfully in the developing countries, at the same time the case for its adoption is stronger there. The pressure for rapid development means that individual rights and the fine points of fair legal procedure are more likely to be disregarded in the interests of speed, efficiency and the broader public interest. The bureaucrats in many former colonies have inherited from their colonial masters an attitude of superiority rather than service, an "insolence of office" which often leads to arbitrariness. And the people are often illiterate and fearful of authority, with little knowledge of their legal and human rights or even of how to articulate a complaint. The office will no doubt require adjustments to fit the special conditions of developing countries, such as allowing complaints to be received orally or by telephone, creating district offices, or having the ombudsman travel to receive complaints.

It may be true, as critics say, that the office is not very well equipped for hunting lions. But it can certainly swat a lot of flies. Even if it should work in the developing countries with only half the effectiveness of the original schemes, its adoption would be well worthwhile.

Footnotes - Chapter 16

1. I should like to thank Mr. J.E. Nebenzahl, the former State Comptroller, for information on his office.

2. Cmnd. 2849 (London, H.M.S.O.), 17-18. See also British Guiana Commission of Inquiry, Racial Problems in the Public Service (Geneva, International Commission of Jurists, Oct. 1965), which reprints the section on the ombudsman from the Report of the Constitutional Commissioner for Mauritius (Prof. S.A. de Smith).

3. Cmnd. 2797, 28-9. See also Constitutional Commission for Mauritius, Report (Mauritius Legislative Assembly Paper, No. 2, 1965).

4. "The Need for an Ombudsman in the Asian and Pacific Region," 26 Bulletin of the International Commission of Jurists (June 1966), 7; United Nations Human Rights Seminar on the Effective Realization of Civil and Political Rights at the National Level, Extracts from Draft Report (Georgetown, Guyana, 1967), 19; Alfred Bexelius, "Background Paper on the Swedish Ombudsman's Institution," (pp. 48, mimeo).

5. Republic of Singapore, Report of the Constitutional Commission, 1966 (Singapore, Government Printer), 18-22.

6. "Digest of Reports," Indian Journal of Public Administration 12 (April-June 1966), 20; for additional commentary on the Vigilance Commission, see earlier issues of the Journal (e.g., 11, 1965, 124).

7. For details of this proposal, see J.B. Monteiro, "Comment," Public Law (Summer 1965), 81-88; see also R.K. Swamy, "The Case for a Permanent Tribunal of Inquiry," Modern Law Review (April 1964), 257-68.

8. Government of India, Administrative Reforms Commission, Interim Report on Problems of Redress of Citizens' Grievances (New Delhi, Oct. 1966), 18 pp. plus an annexure, which is a draft bill. See Appendix in my The Ombudsman.

17

SIMILAR INSTITUTIONS

Because the rise of the positive state in the twentieth century has resulted in a vast bureaucracy in most countries of the world, it is not surprising that a number of them have developed administrative complaint or appeal bodies similar to the ombudsman institution. Some of these are more like it than others, of course. The main measures of their similarity are the degree to which they are independent of the executive and whether they lack the power to make binding decisions. For instance, there is the office of the procurator in the Soviet Union and some other Communist countries, which is controlled by the executive and, in turn, has control powers over the administration. There are agencies like the Administrative Inspection Bureau in Japan, which are part of the executive but have mainly mediating or advisory powers.[1] There are the administrative appeal courts in Western Europe, which are largely independent of the executive, but have the power to make binding legal judicial decisions. There are also the appointed legislative auditors, who as officers of parliament are quite independent of the executive, but who rarely handle complaints from the public. In recent times, there have even developed purely private organizations which take up the cudgels for the wounded "little man" in his fight against the bureaucratic monster.

Executive Complaint Agencies

Complaint agencies which are part of the executive side of government have, of course, existed in many countries for many years. In the United States, examples at the federal level of government are the Inspector General for the army and the Civil Service Commission's complaint office for civil servants. At the local level of government such agencies are often called "complaint bureaus." Related institutions recently created in some American cities are civilian review boards for police administration.

An unusual type of ombudsman-like machinery developed recently in the United States is the use of a federal agency to help with complaints against agencies at the lower levels of government. Under the federal Office of Economic Opportunity, lawyers in the legal services program for the poor not only provided legal aid in court cases but often successfully sued state and local governments on behalf of welfare recipients, migrant workers and other large groups of poor people.

Among the countries of Asia, examples of executive agencies for receiving complaints about maladministration or corruption are the Central Complaints Bureau and the Corrupt Practices Investigation Bureau in Singapore, the Public Complaints Bureau in Malaysia, and the President's Grievance Cell in Pakistan. Similar agencies, already mentioned, are Indian's vigilance commissions, and Tanzania's Permanent Commission of Inquiry, which has been strongly influenced by the ombudsman plan. This influence may also be seen in the appointment of a presidential Complaints Commission for Venezuela in 1969.

Although these institutions do good work in investigating complaints and preventing maladministration, they lack the ombudsman's essential characteric of independence from the executive, because he is an agent of the legislature.

It has been found that a salutary effect of introducing an ombudsman plan is to make executive agencies "complaint conscious," and to encourage them to appoint complaint officers of their own. Such officers are badly needed to handle and quickly satsify most complaints, so that the ombudsman can concentrate on unsatisfied grievances.

Administrative Appeal Courts

Although the common-law countries have some administrative courts, they are for special purposes. In most areas of administration, there is still no right to appeal a decision to an independent body, except to the ordinary courts on a question of law. In several countries of Western Europe, on the other hand, there are comprehensive administrative courts for the general appeal of decisions. These courts are separate from the regular courts and possess varying degrees of comprehensiveness and of independence from the executive. The most comprehensive and independent are found in France and West Germany. The French system, headed by the <u>Conseil</u> <u>d'Etat</u>, is renowned for its independence from the executive authority and for its protection of the individual against simple maladministration as well as abuse of power. An essential difference from the ombudsman is that administrative courts have the power to quash or reverse administrative decisions and therefore have much more formal procedures.

In reviewing administrative action, administrative courts enjoy a number of advantages over ordinary courts.

Among these are cheapness to the complainant, greater ease and informality in lodging a complaint, and the expertise of the judges in administrative matters. However, the transplantation of such courts to the common-law world would require a major revolution in its system of courts and administrative law. Also, because they follow court-like procedures, they suffer from some of the disadvantages of ordinary courts. Sweden has found it desirable to have both a Supreme Administrative Court and ombudsmen. Even in countries which have comprehensive administrative courts, then, an ombudsman system is a valuable addition to the machinery for controlling the administration.

Because of the need for machinery to investigate complaints against the judiciary itself, special ombudsman-like agencies have been created in some countries for the judiciary. An example is the Commission on Judicial Qualifications in California, described in Anderson's Ombudsman for American Government? (see Bibliography). A proposal for similar complaint machinery for the judiciary in Ontario was made in 1969 by the Ontario Royal Commission of Inquiry into Civil Rights.

Legislative Auditors

Among related institutions, the legislative auditor is the closest parallel to the ombudsman in that he is an independent officer of the legislature who investigates and reports on administrative action. Examples are the auditors-general in Commonwealth countries, and the comptroller-general in the United States. Ordinarily they conduct only a post-audit, and have no direct control over the administration. Although they specialize in financial transactions, it has been suggested that they could taken on the functions of an ombudsman by making general administrative inspections and investigating complaints from the public. Some have actually done so, as in Venezuela, Canada and Israel.

In Canada, it was suggested in a broadcast on the ombudsman idea that the public should send administrative grievances to the auditor- general. As a result, for a short time he received a considerable number of complaints by mail. He decided to send those that seemed warranted to the appropriate agency for an explanation, and through the influence of his office successfully secured remedial action in many cases, but did not encourage further complaints.

The outstanding example of a legislative auditor who performs the ombudsman function is the state comptroller of Israel. His position and powers are much like those of an ombudsman. Unlike most legislative auditors, he has a broad power to inspect for not only fiscal regularity but also administrative efficiency, propriety and ethics. Staffed by efficiency experts, his office is a sort of permanent commission on administrative organization. Unlike the American comptroller-general, he has no direct power over the administration. He can only advise, criticize and report to the legislature. However, the inspection function of the state comptroller closely parallels that of the Swedish ombudsmen, and he has a large corps of experienced investigators. Therefore, it is not surprising that the complaint-handling function was left with the state comptroller when specific legal provision was made for it in 1971.

Israel provides an interesting example of the independent development of an institution closely parallel to the ombudsman. If legislative auditors in other countries were to attempt the role of an ombudsman, however, they would probably require a specific legislative mandate to broaden their supervisory powers and to provide for the complaint-handling function.

Private Organizations

In many countries there are private welfare organizations and legal aid bureaus that are willing to take up the cases of helpless individuals who have been unjustly treated by administrative agencies. An interesting example of such an agency in Canada was the organization called "Underdog," which was founded in 1961 by a former newspaper man to help mistreated people. The founder began his operations simply by placing classified advertisements in city newspapers across Canada, offering to help mistreated "underdogs." As his number of cases grew, he enlisted the support of volunteer investigators in the cities from which the complaints came. He also assembled an advisory committee for difficult cases, and began expanding his activities and network of volunteer investigators to other countries. In 1962 the organization received over 1100 allegations of mistreatment. Although it handled any type of case, many were complaints against government administration and many of these were thought to be justified. At my request, the head of Underdog analysed his Canadian complaints against official action and found that in the first eighteen months of operation Underdog had received 173 such complaints, of which 69 had to do with the federal government, 84 were provincial and 20 were municipal.

By 1964 Underdog had expanded its activities into fifteen countries, including the United States. It was only a shoestring organization, however, financed by volunteer contributions and help, and was primarily a one-man show. Its founder's chief weapon for obtaining remedial action was publicity. In fact, his methods for publicizing cases of alleged mistreatment were so unorthodox that they culminated in the spectacular incident mentioned earlier: in the fall of 1964, wishing to dramatize a client's grievance, he threw a milk carton of cow's blood on the floor of the House of Commons; he was promptly jailed, and became popularly known as the "blood bomber." This ridiculous publicity stunt ruined the future usefulness of the organization. Nevertheless, its rapid spread into many other countries is a good indication of the growing need everywhere for additional machinery to investigate individual complaints against both private and public administration.

A similar recent development has been the rapid growth of complaints columns in large daily papers, and of special radio and television programs to receive and investigate individual grievances against the actions of public or private organizations. Some even use the word "ombudsman" in their titles, and some have large staffs which handle hundreds of letters and thousands of phone calls a week. Only the most newsworthy complaints are discussed publicly, and action on the remainder is reported directly to the complainant. Although these columns and programs handle any type of grievance, they play a role surprisingly like that of ombudsmen when investigating complaints against official action. Their main disadvantage, however, is that they have no official power to get at government documents, inspect administrative activities or report to parliament. Also, their coverage of the population is spotty, their budgets vary, and their staffs' knowledge of administrative law is erratic. Nevertheless, the thousands of complaints against official action received each year demonstrate that the job of investigating them is too big for elected representatives to handle by themselves.

Further confirmation that legislators cannot do the whole job is the existence of a private organization in Britiain which developed before the appointment of Britain's parliamentary commissioner. This is the Citizens' Advice Bureaux Service, which offers free information and advice to citizens, and comprises over 400 separate bureaus in nearly all the cities and many of the towns in the United Kingdom. These bureaus are staffed mainly by volunteers but usually have a panel of expert consultants on special subjects. Many of their cases involve administrative action. For serious cases they have a national committee which can deal with the central administration. Like the newspaper complaint columns, however, the emphasis of this organization is more on giving information and advice than on investigating allegations of maladministration or injustice.

Our brief survey of similar complaint machinery in the English-speaking countries and elsewhere, then, indicates that the ombudsman system is unique. Although many of the related institutions have some of its features, none of them possesses all of the advantages of the ombudsman's unusual combination of characteristics.

Footnotes - Chapter 17

1. The institutions in Russia and Japan are described fully in Professor Gellhorn's <u>Ombudsmen and Others</u> (see Bibiliography).

Conclusion

The worldwide discussion of the need for an ombudsman plan has, of course, raised questions about its suitability for countries with varying histories, characteristics and systems of government. Many of the earlier arguments against its transfer were based on the social, legal and constitutional differences between the Nordic countries and those of the Commonwealth, which have the doctrine of ministerial responsibility, or those like the United States, which has a separation of powers between the legislature and the executive. However, the successful adoption of the plan in several Commonwealth countries and its adoption at the state and local levels in the United States have demonstrated its flexibility and have greatly reduced the force of these arguments.

The two most important questions remaining seem to be whether the system can work successfully at the central level in large federal states, and in the difficult circumstances faced by most developing countries. The successful adoption of the plan in Great Britain and France would seem to indicate that earlier fears about its unsuitability for populous countries were unfounded. However, the British and French offices are seriously truncated versions of the plan since they may not receive complaints direct from the public and are restricted to those passed on by members of parliament. This has kept the total work-load of the offices small enough to be manageable. It may be that a full plan in a large country would work better with a collegial complaints commission, as in Austria, or multiple ombudsmen who divide their work by function as in Sweden, or by level as in India, or with separate offices for different administrative activities. It may also require a decentralization of the institution into district offices, or local "mini-ombudsmen" to screen complaints and help with the submission of genuine grievances, as in France and Japan. Some scholars argue that a functional division or decentralization of the institution would cause it to lose its attractive personal touch, which they consider a key to its success. Others, however, including myself, contend that the importance of the personal touch has been exaggerated; far more important is the citizen's faith in the institution's independence and impartiality.

Some unresolved problems concerning the nature and powers of the office are whether the ombudsman should have the power to criticize the decisions made by cabinet ministers

or to review the wisdom of a decision as well as the procedure by which it was made. Others are the amount of publicity that should be given to his office and his investigations, the extent to which he should have access to secret
documents and inspect government agencies on his own
initiative, and whether his jurisdiction should include the
courts, as in Finland and Sweden. More serious problems are
how to keep the ombudsman free from executive influence and
how to make his appointment politically non-partisan in
countries that have a strong tradition of executive and partisan appointment.

In North America the ombudsman idea has become so popular that the word "ombudsman" is used to describe any new
complaint-handling or appeal machinery. Thus, the term Tax
Ombudsmen was used in the bill by U.S. Senators Magnuson and
Long proposing administrative appeal judges. The most serious misapplication of the term has been to complaint officers who are appointed by and responsible to the executive
side of government. Thus in 1971 the U.S. Postmaster General
appointed a so-called postal ombudsman for business. Similarly, several executive complaint officers at the state and
local levels are called ombudsmen. Unfortunately, this usage
is likely to confuse the public and cause them to lose sight
of the important point that a genuine ombudsman is an independent officer of the legislature. Even in non-governmental organizations, new complaint officers are being called
ombudsmen. The idea has been proposed for trade unions and
business corporations, to prevent union officials or employ-
ers from dealing arbitrarily with workers and thus to promote due process of law in private administration. While
these applications of the idea have great value, the use of
the term ombudsman in the titles of the offices is confusing, since these offices often bear little resemblance to
the original parliamentary ombudsman. The indiscriminate
use of the word may rob it of its essential meaning.

It is perhaps already too late for the popular use of
the term to be restricted to an officer responsible only to
the legislature. If so, writers who refer to other kinds of
grievance officers should be careful to use an appropriate
qualifying word - executive ombudsman, university ombudsman,
newspaper ombudsman, etc. At the same time, proponents and
legislators, simply because it is a new word and may at
first seem strange, should not shrink from using it as a
formal title for genuine ombudsmen. And they should insist
that it be given only to politically independent grievance
officers. Otherwise, confusion is likely to prevail, and
many so-called ombudsman will end up in the vest pockets of

chief executives, or as advocates for the administration's point of view.

Through the growing public popularity of the ombudsman idea, there is thus a sense in which it may become its own worst enemy. Any kind of new complaint or appeal officer in any kind of organization is now likely to be mistakenly dubbed an ombudsman in order to gain popular support for his activities. It is becoming all too easy to lose sight of the basic features of the original ombudsman systems. These features are summed up in my following definition of the institution:

1) It is an independent and non-partisan office of the legislature, provided for in the constitution or by law, which supervises the administration;
2) it deals with specific complaints from the public against administrative injustice and maladministration; and
3) it has the power to investigate, criticize and publicize, but not to reverse, administrative action.

To avoid public confusion in discussing the ombudsman idea, the use of the term "ombudsman" should therefore be restricted to institutions that have all of these features. Otherwise, the vital importance of one or other of them may be forgotten when so-called ombudsman plans are being proposed.

Requirements for Success

An assessment of the experience with ombudsman offices around the world indicates that there are five key requirements for the office to be fully successful.

The first requirement is that complaints must be allowed to go direct to the ombudsman's office rather than being filtered through a member of parliament as in Britain and France. It is an important principle of administrative justice that a citizen should be a party in his own case, and he should not be required first to appeal to a partisan member of parliament whose objectivity may be in question. The fact that the ombudsmen in Britain and France have a very small number of complaints in proportion to population compared with other plans, indicates that the need there is not being fully met.

The second requirement is that the office must be widely known and easily accessible. The occupational disease of ombudsmen is an inadequate pubicizing of their services for fear of being overloaded and thus being accused of the same kind of delay and red-tape that they are supposed to be curing in the administration. Studies have shown that even after an ombudsman office has been in existence for many years, a large proportion of the population have never heard of it. Ombudsmen must therefore take every opportunity to publicize their services through the media and must make their services easily accessible throughout the country by means of regional offices, frequent visits to outlying areas and free long distance calls from complainants.

Third, the scope of an ombudsman plan must be broad. It ought to include all types of administrative agencies and all levels of government, because appointed officials everywhere fall prey to the arrogance of the office. As we have seen in Italy and Switzerland, where a plan is implemented only at one level of government, the ombudsman is likely to be overloaded with complaints against administration at the other levels.

Fourth, an ombudsman must be given strong powers, short of having the power to make binding decisions. He must have the power to criticize the actions of ministers and the use of administrative discretion where it has been clearly unreasonable, and should not be restricted only to cases of maladministration as in Britain. He should have the power to initiate his own investigations, to demand all relevant information and documents, and to recommend the amendment of regulations and laws. Where the administration has refused his recommendation on a particular case which is pressing, he should have the power to publicize this before he makes his annual report to parliament. There should also be a special committee of the legislature to consider his reports, take up his recommendations, and see that action is taken on them.

The fifth - and probably most important - requirement is that the office of ombudsman must be absolutely independent from the executive government and from partisan influence. This must be ensured through the provisions for appointment, tenure, salary, staffing and budgeting. In order to protect the fundamental nature of the office from this point of view, the basic provisions for it should be contained in a country's constitution, as in Denmark and in the new constitutions of Portugal, Spain and many developing countries.

If all or most of these requirements are not met, the office can easily be turned into a weak one which provides the form but not much substance. Although it may do good work in remedying a small number of minor cases, it may not be known widely enough to reach all segments of the public and may be unable to remedy serious cases of administrative injustice. Advocates of the plan in countries considering its adoption would therefore do well to press hard for a plan that meets all of these requirements.

In a country that has an authoritarian regime or widespread corruption, the plan may work with moderate success to solve minor problems, but it cannot cure a major disease in the working of government and should not be expected to accomplish miracles. Giving the office objectives and a title that are too ambitious, as appears to have been the case in India, Portugal and Spain, may lead the pubic to expect more of the office than it can deliver and hence lose faith in it.

Although many types of related institutions and organizations have arisen for remedying complaints against modern administrative action, the ombudsman institution has a unique combination of characteristics that give it advantages over all other types. The most important of these is the independence from the executive side of government, achieved by making it an agency of the legislature. Its prestige and its powers to investigate, to inspect and to publicize give it a strength which non-governmental organizations and even members of a legislature cannot match. At the same time, because it does not have the power to control, it does not interfere unduly with the administrative process. For these reasons, the ombudsman plan will continue to spread throughout the democratic world.

BIBLIOGRAPHY OF MAIN PUBLICATIONS

The literature on the ombudsman is now vast, as is the number of books on schemes in single countries. This bibliography therefore includes only the most important comparative books published in English.

In addition to the materials listed below, readers should know about the publications of the International Ombudsman Institute (located at the Law Centre, University of Alberta, Edmonton, Canada, T6G 2H5). Particularly valuable are the annual Ombudsman and Other Complaint-Handling Systems Survey and the bi-monthly Newsletter, which give a comprehensive review of developments around the world. The Survey was founded by Bernard Frank, former chairman of the International Bar Association's Ombudsman Committee, and is published in conjunction with this committee. The Institute also publishes The Ombudsman Journal (which began in September 1981), the proceedings of the International Ombudsman Conferences, a series of Occasional Papers and other studies, and a comprehensive annual bibliography. These publications, or a complete list of them, may be ordered direct from the Institute at the above address. Also, the bibliography is consolidated and computerized, and the Institute will make specific bibliographic searches on request.

Anderson, Stanley V., ed., Ombudsmen for American Government? (Englewood Cliffs, N.J.: Prentice-Hall, 1968), 181 pp. Essays prepared for the 1967 American Assembly.

Caiden, Gerald, ed., International Handbook of the Ombudsman (Westport, CT.: Greenwood Press, 1982). A comprehensive survey in two volumes.

Gellhorn, Walter, Ombudsmen and Others: Citizens' Protectors in Nine Countries (Cambridge: Harvard University Press, 1966), 448 pp. Includes Denmark, Finland, New Zealand, Norway, Sweden, Yugoslavia, Poland, Soviet Union and Japan.

Gellhorn, Walter, When Americans Complain: Governmental Grievance Procedures (Cambridge: Harvard University Press, 1966), 239 pp.

Jain, M.P., Lokpal: Ombudsman in India (New Delhi: Academic Books, 1970), 332 pp. Analysis of proposals for India; includes a survey of ombudsman plans in Scandinavia, New Zealand and United Kingdom.

The Ombudsman or Citizens' Defender: A Modern Institution, a symposium in Annals of the American Academy of Political and Social Science 377 (May 1968), 138 pp. Has fourteen essays, on Sweden, the spread of the institution, Finland, Norway, Denmark, New Zealand, Britain, Communist Europe, the Mediterranean area, and four on the U.S.

Rowat, Donald C., ed., The Ombudsman: Citizens' Defender (London: Allen and Unwin; Toronto: University of Toronto Press; Stockholm: Norstedt; 2nd ed. 1968), 384 pp. Essays by 29 authors; 2nd ed. has a Preface on worldwide developments, and additions to the Appendix on Britain, Alberta, India, and the U.S. (including Hawaii).

Stacey, Frank A., Ombudsmen Compared (Oxford: Clarendon Press, 1978), 256 pp. Compares the ombudsman plans in Scandinavia, Canada, France and the United Kingdom.

Weeks, Kent M., Ombudsmen Around the World: A Comparative Chart (Berkeley: Institute of Governmental Studies, 2nd ed. 1978), 163 pp. Compares key aspects of 38 ombudsman offices.

Wyner, Alan J., ed., Executive Ombudsmen in the United States (Berkeley: Institute of Governmental Studies, 1973), 315 pp.

NOTE ON AUTHOR

Donald C. Rowat is a graduate of the University of Toronto and Columbia University. He has gained a reputation as a leading expert on municipal government, laws on access to official documents and the ombudsman, and has edited The Ombudsman: Citizens' Defender (London, Toronto and Stockholm, 1968). He is author of The Canadian Municipal System (Toronto, 1969) and Your Local Government (Toronto, 1955, 2nd ed. 1975). He has also edited Basic Issues in Public Administration (New York, 1961), The Government of Federal Capitals (Toronto, 1973), Administrative Secrecy in Developed Countries (London and New York, 1979) and International Handbook on Local Government Reorganization (Westport, CT, 1980), and is currently editing Public Administration in the Developed Democracies, a comparative survey of twenty countries.

Dr. Rowat is at present Professor of Political Science at Carleton University, Ottawa, Canada.

INDEX

Abel, Albert, 64
Adelaide, 140
Adenauer, Chancellor, 44
Administrative Conference of the United States, 96
Administrative Counsellors, Japan, 157
Administrative Inspection Bureau of the Administrative
  Management Agency, Japan, 157, 160
Administrative Ombudsman Experimentation Act, United States, 87
Administrative Reforms Commission, India, 164, 165
Administrative Review Council, Australia, 140
Administrative Review Tribunal, Australia, 140
Alaska, 85, 87, 89, 90
Alberta, 96, 109, 110, 111, 112, 133
Alberta Bar Association, 108
Allen and Unwin, v
American Assembly, 86
American Bar Association, 86
American Ombudsman Foundation, 87
Anchorage, Alaska, 85
Anderson, Stanley, 39, 85, 86, 87, 107, 175
Andhra Pradesh, 166
Ananda, M.G., 141
Article 54, Constitution of Spain, 149
Aspin, Congressman, 86
Atlanta, GA., 92
Australia, 64, 78, 133, 134, **139-141**
Australian National University, Canberra, 140
Austria, 61, 97, 124, 134, 141, **145-148**, 159, 181

Bangladesh, 168
Bauer, Franz, 145, 146
Belgium, 156
Berkeley, Cal., 92
Bexelius, A., 4, 6, 7, 11, 83, 89, 123, 132, 133, 171
Bihar, 166
Bill C-7 (Canada), 118
Bill C-52 (Canada), 119, 120, 122
Bingham, T., 91
Bophuthatswana, 167
Bophuthatswana Control Commission (Ombudsman) Act, 167
Bras, Colonel Costa, 143
Bremen, 152
Brisbane, 140
Britain, 68, 71, 116, 122, 132, 133, **135-139**, 142, 148,
  150, 157, 177, 181, 183, 184; see also United Kingdom

Dalhousie University, Halifax, 110
Davies, J., 159
Dayton, Ohio, 87
Dayton-Montgomery County, Ohio, 90
Defence Force Ombudsman, Australia, 141
Defender of the People, Spain, 149, 150
Denmark, iv, 15, **31-34**, 46, 55, 67, 69, 71, 89, 97, 100, 132, 148, 184
Der Spiegel, 42
Detroit, Mich., 92
Dixon, Oliver, 139
Dominica, 168
Dwyer, P., 89

Finland, iv, **15-28**, 29, 32, 46, 52, 68, 70, 71, 116, 131, 133, 182
Flavin, Francis, 85
Flemington, Ross, 110, 113
Flint, 90, 92
Florence, 154
France, 61, 96, 103, 122, 134, **141-143**, 146,157, 174, 181, 183
Frank, Bernard, vi, 86
Freedom of Education Act of 1982, Australia, 140
Friedmann, Karl, 110, 127
Fruilia-Venezia Guilia, 154

Gandhi, Indira, 166
Gellhorn, W., 83, 85, 89, 90, 91, 160
General Counsel for Grievances, Australia, 140
Germany, Federal Republic of, see West Germany
Ghana, 167
Gibson, Mayor, 91
Gil-Delgado, A., 159
Godinho, José de Magalhaes, 143
Guam, Territory of, 85
Guyana, iv, 133, 162, 163

Haifa, 161
Haller, Walter, 150
Hansen, Inger, 125
Harvard Student Legislative Research Bureau, 89
Hawaii, iv, 89, 90, 133
Hébert, J., 99
Heinemann, Gustav, 152
Heye, Vice-Admiral, 42, 45
Hiden, Mikael, 15
Holt, Prime Minister, Australia, 140
Hong Kong, 163

Mache, Italy, 154
Madhya Pradesh, 166
Magnuson, Senator, 85, 182
Maharashtra, India, 166
Maizière, General, 45
Malaysia, 163, 174
Maloney, Arthur, 110, 112
Maltby, George, 110, 112, 114
Manitoba, 108, 109, 110, 111, 114
Marceau, Louis, 110, 113
Mauritius, 133, 162, 163
Mauritius Constitutional Conference, 162
McLellan, George, 110, 112, 113
McNeil, Murrell, 85
Médiateur, 141
Melbourne, 140
Mensch und Staat, 152
Menzies, Prime Minister of Australia, 140
Messmer, Prime Minister of France, 141
Michigan Bar Association, 92
Milne, A.G., 127
Minister of Finance, Ireland, 149
Minister of Home Affairs, Netherlands, 148
Minister of Interior, Netherlands, 148
Minister of Justice, Netherlands, 148
Mitchell, J.D.B., 64, 65
Monteiro, J., 171
Montreal, 98
Mortati, C., 159
Mount Allison University, Sackville, N.B., 110

Nassau County, N.Y., 83
National Health Service Act, Scotland, 138
National Ombudsman Act, Netherlands, 148
Nebenzahl, J., 171
Nebraska, 84
Neighborhood City Halls, New York, 89
Netherlands, 141, 147, 148
New Brunswick, 104, 109, 111, 113, 115, 125, 133
Newfoundland, 104, 108, 109, 110, 111, 125
New York (City), 92
New York (State), 87
New Zealand, iv, 3, 15, 29, 31, **34-38**, 46, 58, 61, 64,
    67, 68, 70, 89, 97, 102, 109, 111, 116, 118, 120, 121,
    124, 131, 132, 133, 136, 139, 144, 147, 163, 164
Nigeria, 168
Northern Ireland, 136, 138
Northern Ireland Act 1974, 139
North-Rhine Westphalia, 152
Nova Scotia, 104, 108, 110, 111, 115

Procedures Act, Administrative, 96; American Administrative, 103, 108
Provedor de Justica, Portugal, 143, 144
Provisional Commission on Administrative Reform, Japan, 157
Public Complaints Commission, Nigeria, 168
Public Petitions Committee, Sri Lanka, 168
Public Service Organization Review Group, Ireland, 149
Public Complaints Bureau, Malaysia, 174
Puerto Rico, Commonwealth of, 85
Puglia, Italy, 154
Punjab Administrative Reforms Commission, 164

Queensland, Australia, 140

Rajasthan, India, 164, 166
Rang, J., 148
Reuss, Congressman, 82, 83, 85, 87, 109
Rhineland-Palatinate, 152, 153
Richardson, Jack, 140
Robles, A., 150
Rossler, Johannes, 153
Rotterdam, 147, 148
Rowat, Donald C., vii, 39, 159, 171, 189
Royal Canadian Mounted Police, 110
Russia, 179
Ryan, Representative, 87

Salzburg, 145
San Francisco, 92
Saskatchewan, 107, 108, 110
Schei, Andreas, 31
Scotland, 71, 138
Seattle, 87, 91
Seattle-King County, 90, 91
Senate, American, 7
Shawcross, Lord, 49
Singapore, 163, 171, 174
Sheppard, C.A., 73
Smith, Arthur, 118
Smith, Harry, 110
Smith, S.A. de, 171
Social Sciences and Humanities Research Council of Canada, vi
Solicitor General, Canada, 125
Solomon Islands, 167
South Australia, 140
South Carolina, 88
Spain, 134, 141, **149-150**, 184, 185
Sri Lanka, 168
Steenbeek, J., 148
Steiger, Representative, 87